The Music Producer's Guide to Compression

The Music Producer's Guide To Compression

Published by Stereo Output Limited, company number 11174059

ISBN number 9781999600372

Copyright © Ashley Hewitt 2021

Table of Contents

Introduction

Compression can make or break a piece of music.

Used correctly, compression will give your tracks verve, energy and focus. It will remove unwanted variations in intensity and pull different sonic elements together, making your tracks sound coherent and professional. When used poorly - or not at all - the tracks you make will inevitably fall flat.

Compression touches every facet of recorded music. It is the main reason why a Bowie LP from the 1970s sounds so fundamentally different to that same LP on Spotify, and why contemporary EDM can be such an intensely visceral experience.

Learning about compression and how to use it in the right way is an essential part of the modern music producer's education. You will not get far in your music production without a good working knowledge of how to make proper use of this powerful effect.

In this book we'll explore both the traditional functions of compression and the outer edges of its use in contemporary settings. It is not a prescriptive approach filled with rules and formulae, but a useful guide to help you to utilise compression across a broad range of music production contexts.

As you work your way through these pages, you will be encouraged to undertake your own creative approach to the process of compression, gaining vital first-hand experience in the use of compressors within your own projects.

By the end of this book, you will understand:

1. What compression is, and why producers use it.
2. The history of compression.
3. The primary functions of all compressors.
4. The secondary functions of many compressors.
5. The fundamental techniques for using compressors.
6. Classic compression techniques.
7. The difference between compressing downwards and compressing upwards.
8. Examples of compression in action in the studio.
9. Fun ways of using compressors to bring a sense of novelty and uniqueness to your music productions.

Chapter 1: The Fundamentals of Dynamic Range Compression

1.1: The Nature of Sound Intensity

Compression is classed as a *dynamic effect*. What this means is that it modifies an audio signal by causing changes to the sound intensity.

Compression was first developed during the advent of military signal technology, when flattening the amplitude of signals was essential to ensure their consistency, such as keeping audio signals at an audible volume whether the speaker was shouting or whispering. Its application to radar technology ensured that returning signals were of amplitude that could be read without mistakes. The subsequent transition of compression to the music studio was a natural progression, where it proved a useful means for adding colour, depth, warmth and punch to a sound.

When understanding compression within the context of music production, the key property we need to focus on is the *intensity* of sound. Because of the way our ears perceive sound intensity, this is often equated with the sound volume.

As you probably already know, the vibrations of a sound source create a pressure wave that consists of alternating layers of high and low pressure. The human ear detects these changes of pressure and they are heard as sound by the listener.

Here now is an important point: the bigger the deviation of pressure, the greater the intensity of the sound. This is shown in Figure 1.1 below, where wave **a** depicts a sound wave of higher intensity than **b**. Notice the difference in their respective amplitudes - the relative height and depth of the waves themselves. The pressure deviation of sound wave **a** is large, and this is reflected in the large amplitude of the sound wave. In sound wave **b** this pressure deviation is lower and is reflected in the lower amplitude of the sound wave:

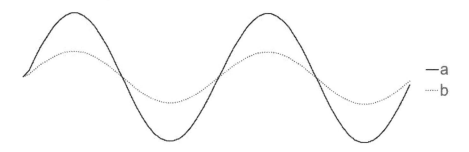

Figure 1.1: Two sound waves. Sound wave **a** is of higher intensity than sound wave **b**.

Sound intensity is measured using the Decibel scale, which begins with the quietest sound that the human ear can register. This lowest point is known as the auditory threshold and is conveniently set at 0dB. To put this into perspective, the sound of a light leaf rustling nearby would be roughly 10dB, whilst a whisper would correspond to about 20dB.

When studying the Decibel scale, bear in mind that it is logarithmic. What this means is that an increase of 10dB corresponds to a doubling in the perceived level of volume. A sound intensity of 30dB would therefore be heard to be twice as loud as a sound intensity of 20dB. The need for using a logarithmic scale becomes evident when we consider that the intensity of the sound of a jet taking off is literally over a billion times louder than the sound of a pin dropping on a hard wooden floor.

For music producers, sound intensity is a serious business, not just in terms of music production, but also our wellbeing. Long term exposure to sounds of too high an intensity can permanently damage our hearing. It might surprise you to learn that this damage can occur from prolonged exposure to sounds as low as 70dB, which is far below the human threshold of pain (at around 130-140dB). Always take care of your sense of hearing! It is your greatest asset as a music producer.

Table 1.1 lists some general intensity levels to help you develop a basic idea of the dB scale:

Table 1.1: The intensity levels of different sounds.

Sound	dB
Light leaf rustling	10
Normal conversation	40-60
A passing car at 10 meters	60-80
Jack hammer	100
Jet engine	150
Stun grenade	160

Now that we have a convenient way to measure sound intensity, let's consider some additional concepts that are useful to understand when studying compression. The first of these is the concept of dynamic range.

1.2: Dynamic Range

Hearing a sound depends upon two factors: the loudness of the sound itself and the background level of sound (also known as the noise floor). Put simply, you cannot hear a leaf rustling in a storm, and you cannot hear a quiet conversation at a rock concert.

This leads us to an important observation. The level of the sound alone is not the main factor - it is the level of the sound relative to the noise floor that determines whether or not it can be heard. The difference in intensity between the noise floor and the individual sound is called the *dynamic range* (not to be confused with the related, but separate concept of 'dynamic range' used to describe the expressive difference between the quietest and the loudest sounds within a musical composition).

To understand the usefulness of the concept of dynamic range, consider the following scenario. Imagine you had a recording of a small crowd of people talking to each other. Some individuals might be speaking fairly loudly, around say 60–75 dB, whilst others could be whispering in the 10–15 dB range. How would you set about balancing this recording so that both the loud conversation and the whispers were equally audible?

You would use a compressor.

Through use of a compressor, the level of the loudest conversation could be brought down and the level of the whispers could be raised. The result would be a recording with less dynamic range, but one with more viable uses.

To illustrate this point in a more general way, look at the two waveforms shown in Figure 1.2. Do you notice how some parts of the waveform are taller than others, meaning they are louder? This difference between them defines the dynamic range of that sound, which extends from the shortest (quietest) to the tallest (loudest) parts of the waveform:

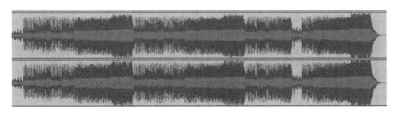

Figure 1.2: A waveform with normal dynamic range, from the quiet to the loud.

If we were to apply a compression effect to this sound, the resulting waveform would look now like this:

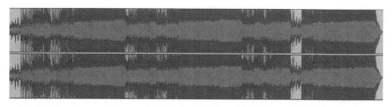

Figure 1.3: A waveform with less dynamic range due to compression.

When we compare the two illustrated waveforms, you will see that the loudest parts of the sound have stayed at a similar level, but in Figure 1.2. the quieter parts have become much louder. This is because the compression used has reduced the dynamic range.

Let's now consider a further concept that is essential to our understanding of dynamic range: transients.

1.3: Transients

Transients are the high-amplitude, short-duration sounds that occur right at the beginning of a sound. They are important for recognition and identification of the sound source, and they are also the biggest contributor to dynamic range.

In Figure 1.4, for example, you can see the waveform of a snare drum hit.

Figure 1.4: The waveform of a snare drum hit.

The big peak right at the start of the sound is the transient.

Transient

Figure 1.5: The waveform of a snare drum hit, with an arrow showing the transient.

Due to the variety of ways in which a sound might be produced, instruments will generate different transients. A synthesizer stab, for example, might have a soft, but still prominent transient, as shown in Figure 1.6:

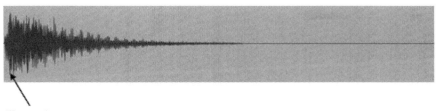

Transient

Figure 1.6: The waveform of a synthesizer stab, with an arrow pointing to the transient.

Having seen how transients occur in individuals sounds, let's look at an example in which numerous sounds occur in succession, such as a two-bar drum loop.

In Figure 1.7, we can immediately see that our two-bar drum loop contains many transients:

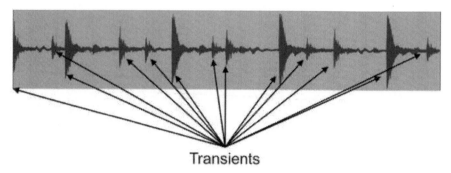

Transients

Figure 1.7: The waveform of a two-bar drum loop, with arrows pointing to the transients.

This shows us that transients are the main drivers of dynamic range, which in turn leads to an important observation: *because transients are the loudest part of a sound, they are disproportionately affected by compression.*

It is therefore paramount to remember that *compression often only affects transients*, and these transients comprise just a small proportion of the overall waveform. Compression of a drum track for example, will principally involve compression of the transients produced by the surface being struck, leaving the remainder of the waveform largely untouched. Similarly, compression of the sound from an acoustic guitar will principally compress the transients that result from the strings being plucked, allowing much of the ensuing vibration through.

Chapter 2: The Basics of Compression

2.1: The Compression Machine

In order to focus on the machinery of compression itself, let's begin by looking at the process of dynamic range reduction in reverse, rather as if we were going to invent a compressor from scratch.

Using the examples from the previous chapter, we can surmise that there are two possible ways to get from the sound shown in Figure 2.1 - with its many variations in intensity - to the more even-looking waveform of the same sound, shown in Figure 2.2:

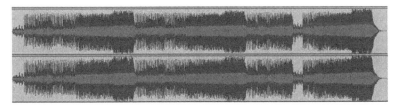

Figure 2.1: A copy of Figure 1.2 showing an uncompressed signal with a high dynamic range.

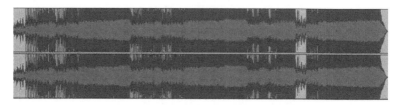

Figure 2.2: A copy of Figure 1.3 showing a compressed signal with little
dynamic range.

Assuming that the loudest parts of the uncompressed waveform
are the peaks, we could increase the intensity of the troughs to be
roughly equal to these peaks. This is called upwards compression.
Alternatively, we could reduce the intensity of the peaks so that
they more closely match those of the troughs and then apply gain
to increase the level of the whole sound. This is known as
downwards compression.

Both techniques form an important part of the machinery of
modern compression. Table 2.1 summarises the main differences
between the two approaches:

Table 2.1: The difference between upwards compression and downward
  compression.

Upwards compression	Downwards compression
Increasing the intensity of the troughs closer to the peaks.	Reducing the intensity of the peaks, then increasing the overall gain.
Difficult without a computer	Can be done using simple electronics.
Risk of increasing the volume of undesired noises (e.g. tape hiss, mouth pops, etc.) if using analog recording media..	Has very little effect on the quieter sounds.

This brings us to an important question: what functions would a compressor have to possess, in order to be able to perform both upwards and downwards compression?

Firstly, the compressor would need to be capable of detecting the intensity of the signals that pass through it. Secondly, it would have to be able to reduce the intensity of any signals that exceeded the threshold we'd set for it. Thirdly, a mechanism for adjusting that required threshold would need to be available.

Finally, it should allow us to apply gain, in other words, increase the intensity of the whole signal after downwards compression had been applied.

Our basic requirement diagram is depicted in Figure 2.3:

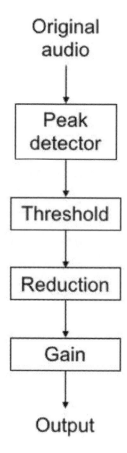

Figure 2.3: The requirements of a basic compressor.

During the history of compression design, compressors have sought to accomplish these essential functions in a variety of different and ingenious ways, and we'll explore a few of these below.

2.2: The History of Compression

Having been expanded from its initial military uses, musical compression first appeared as a tool in AM radio, as a means by which to maintain clarity and listening comfort. If a broadcast sound breaches a certain level, it will cause the signal to over-modulate and the listeners will hear an unpleasant distortion, something radio broadcasters were understandably keen to avoid. Compression has also seen significant use across television broadcasting to create uniformity in the audio levels of TV programmes. Whether a character was whispering or shouting, they could easily be heard on a television set whose volume had already been set by the user.

From there, compression gradually made its way into the recording studio, where producers found that it not only automated the challenging process of 'riding' a fader (moving sound faders up and down quickly, to compensate for the natural dynamic range of a recording) but also added a certain degree of natural warmth to the sound.

In section 2.1 we saw that a compressor would need to be able to detect the intensity of the input signal, apply gain reduction, and trigger according a user-set threshold. Compressors have employed a variety of different approaches to meet these functions over the history of their development.

2.2.1: Tube Compressors (a.k.a. Vari-Mu)

During the 1950s, the ingenious use of vacuum tube amplifiers provided a technique of compression that proved ideal for musical purposes. They were used primarily as sound amplifiers, and the extent of the amplification could be modified by varying the amount of voltage sent to them.

By duplicating the signal, and then measuring the intensity of that duplicate, the intensity of the signal could drive the voltage sent to the tubes. This compressed the signal, as depicted in Figure 2.4:

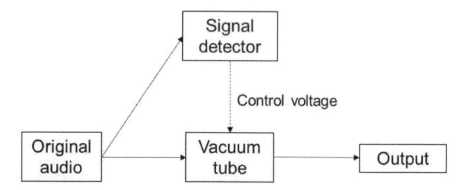

Figure 2.4: The basic signal flow of a tube compressor.

Because this method relied on the speed with which the vacuum tube could respond to the control voltage, these compressors were comparatively slow to respond to transients. This meant that disproportionately loud sounds - such as snare hits - often slipped through the net. On the plus side however, these vacuum tubes added a small amount of warm, pleasant distortion to the sound, much in the same way that guitar amplifiers did.

This desirable sound quality began the trend of compressors being utilised not only for their primary function of modifying the intensity of audio signals, but also their secondary attribute of affecting the overall aesthetics of the sound in an agreeable way.

One of the most famous tube compressors was the Fairchild 660/670, a 30kg behemoth decked out with 20 valves. Taking 30 minutes or more just to warm up, it was renowned in its day for the impressive warmth that it lent to sound. This quality significantly contributed to The Beatles' signature sound, from the 1964 Hard Day's Night sessions onwards. A Fairchild compressor is depicted in Figure 2.5:

Figure 2.5: A Fairchild compressor.

These compressors are still revered to this day, so much so, that despite their fragile internal components, a fully working Fairchild can fetch upwards of £20,000. In fact, at the time of writing, brand new Fairchild clones are available on the market for upwards of £10,000.

2.2.2: Optical Compressors

Most early compressors measured the intensity of incoming audio signals by way of voltage - the more intense the signal, the higher the voltage.

Optical compressors meanwhile took a tangential approach; they transformed a copy of the audio signal into light. They did this by amplifying the audio signal to the voltage range required to power up a lightbulb. The intensity of this light was then detected by a photocell. The more light the cell received, the more gain reduction was applied.

A well-known example of this type of compressor was the Teletronix LA-2A. It used an extremely sensitive, military grade photoresistor that had almost infinite resistance in the dark. The presence of light caused that resistance to drop, allowing it to control gain reduction within the circuit.

Using a light cell had both advantages and disadvantages. Think about operating an incandescent lightbulb; there is a slight delay between turning the light on and the filament illuminating, and another brief delay between turning it off and the bulb going out. In terms of optical compression this meant that there was always a minor delay between a peak in the music and the compressor activating. Many producers perceive this slightly delayed response to the peaks as musical and expressive. Just like tube compressors, however, the slow response of optical compressors meant that they often failed to react to transients in a timely manner, and could sometimes allow quite harsh transients through, uncompressed. Two of these wonderful compressors can be seen in Figure 2.6:

Figure 2.6: A couple of Teletronix optical compressors in an effects rack.

One further feature (or flaw, depending on your perspective) of an optical compressor was its nonlinear response; the bigger the peaks fed into the compressor, the more quickly it reduced the amount of compression from its highest point. This meant that over an 8dB gain reduction, the compression dropped off faster on the first four decibels than the last four, making transients of higher intensity sound punchier and transients of lower intensity sound more relaxed, exaggerating the performer's natural playing.

The difference between a linear and a nonlinear response is shown in Figure 2.7:

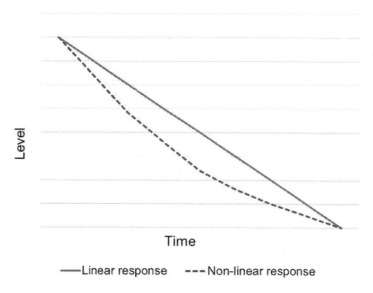

Figure 2.7: The difference between a linear and a nonlinear response. Notice how a linear response is in a straight line, creating a proportionate response, whereas the nonlinear response is curved, creating a response that isn't always proportionate.

The basic circuitry of optical compressors is shown in Figure 2.8:

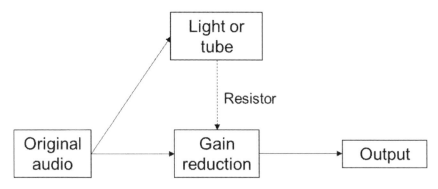

Figure 2.8: The simplified signal flow of an optical compressor.

One fascinating quirk in the manufacture of the earliest optical compressors was that each light-dependent resistor was slightly different to another. Manufacturers who built optical compressors had to buy in large quantities of resistors and test each one, selecting only the few that possessed the right qualities. The remainder were discarded. This variability meant that each compressor was unique in its behaviour and nonlinearity. It is this distinctiveness that has made vintage optical compressors highly desirable to modern producers.

2.2.3: FET Compressors

Field Effect Transistors emerged in the mid-1960s. They could be made to replicate the behaviour of a variable resistor in response to a control voltage - in other words, they could compress sound.

FETs, however, could respond far more quickly to peaks in intensity than light cells or tubes, which gave them a warm, aggressive, sound. This can be heard on Phil Collins' 1981 hit *In The Air Tonight*, accentuating the aggressive reverb effect of the drums.

 Due to their unique circuitry, FET compressors added slight harmonic distortions to a sound. This contributed colour, warmth and a fair amount of noise, to the extent that studio producers looking for an extra edge often chose to record music through FET compressors without applying compression, simply to take advantage of these effects. The UA 1176, one of the most famous FET compressors, is shown in Figure 2.9:

Figure 2.9: A UA 1176 FET compressor. Image courtesy of wing_clipper on Flickr.
https://www.flickr.com/photos/wing_clipper/7213583084/

2.2.4: VCA Compressors

By the early 1970s, transistors had begun taking hold in the electronics market. Transistors were cheaper and faster than their predecessors. One of their applications was in audio compression, in this case by the creation of VCA compressors.

VCA stood for Voltage Controlled Amplifier, and VCA compressors became known for their practicality. Thanks to VCA compressors' circuitry, gain reduction became entirely controllable, predictable, and nonlinear, which meant that VCA compressors were tools of precision. Their attack and release times were more responsive than their predecessors, which made them ideal when a producer was looking to control the dynamics of a sound without adding colour.

VCA compressors became a standard for cheap, reliable compression and can still often be found in many hardware studios or within racks at live gigs. The cheapest models of hardware VCA compressor can be bought for less than £100, providing a great entry point for those who want compression within their hardware studio without spending a fortune on vintage equipment.

Figure 2.10 depicts a Waldorf cmp1, a Eurorack-compatible compressor, currently available for only £161 at the time of writing:

Figure 2.10: A Waldorf cmp1 VCA compression module.

2.2.5: Digital Compressors

With the advent of computer technology, digital compressors came rapidly to the fore - sometimes as hardware compressors in studios, but mainly as software programs within Digital Audio Workstation (DAW) software.

Being software programs, digital compressors are capable of a completely clean, un-coloured signal.

Examples of well-known software digital compressors include Empirical Labs' *Arousor*, Klanghelm's *MJUC*, and Softube's *CL-1B*. The focus of this book, however, will be on compressors that can either be downloaded for free, or are freely available as part of popular DAW packages, such as Logic Pro X's compressor, depicted in Figure 2.11:

Figure 2.11: Logic Pro X's built-in digital compressor.

In addition to modern digital compression, Logic Pro X's built-in compressor is able to simulate all the vintage compression types described so far, including optical, FET and VCA. This is very useful when looking to experiment with different compression types, since producers do not always want clean, clinical results.

Whilst some professional producers would be able to tell the difference between Logic's simulation of vintage compressors and the real thing, most of us would be unable to do so in a blindfold test. It is a miracle that *all* compressor types, from the vintage to the modern, are simulated within this single unit, which comprises just one small part of a reasonably priced software package.

The advent of digital compression opens up a huge range of different options available to a typical producer, with a variety of different compression methods you can harness.

Table 2.2 shows a summary of the compression types listed in this Chapter, which should help inform your decision:

Table 2.2: A summary table of the key attributes of different compression types.

Name	Speed	Flexibility	Behaviour	Colouring
Tube (aka vari-mu)	Medium	Some	Non-linear	Lots
Optical	Slow	Little	Non-linear	Lots
VCA	Fast	Lots	Linear	Little
FET	Fast	Little	Linear	Lots
Digital	Fast	Lots	Linear	Variable

Chapter 3: The Functions of a Compressor

3.1: Threshold and Ratio

Have you ever looked at a compressor and wondered what the controls actually do, what effect they're going to have on your music, and how to harness those effects with precision? If so, this chapter will explain everything you need to know.

The two most important controls on a compressor are Threshold and Ratio, and it is worth taking the time to thoroughly acquaint yourself with the way that they work.

By setting the Threshold level, you inform the compressor of the intensity of signal at which you want it to begin working. Anything below that threshold level will pass through unaffected, and anything above the Threshold level will be compressed. In other words, the lower the Threshold, the more the signal gets compressed; the higher the Threshold, the more the signal passes through without compression being applied to it.

Ratio is the extent to which you want the compressor to reduce the intensity of anything above the level set by your Threshold. It is a mathematical ratio, so when it is set to a low setting, little compression is applied to the signal. When it is set to a high setting, a lot of compression is applied.

Table 3.1 and Figure 3.1 explain compression Ratios.

Imagine a transient arriving that is 6dB over the set Threshold. The 2:1 Ratio will reduce it by 3dB, a 4:1 Ratio will reduce it by 4.5dB and an infinite Ratio by 6dB, as shown in Table 3.1.

Table 3.1: The change in intensity driven by different Ratios assuming a transient 6dB over the Threshold.

Ratio	Change in intensity
1:1 (i.e. none)	0dB
2:1	-3dB
3:1	-4dB
4:1	-4.5dB
Infinite	-6dB

An alternative way of looking at this is depicted in Figure 3.1:

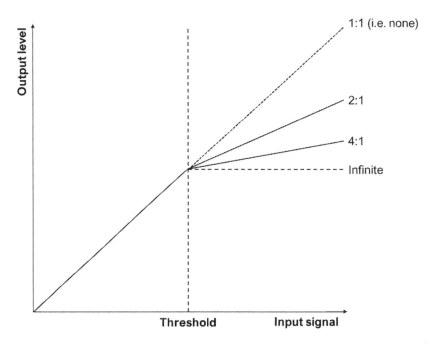

Figure 3.1: An alternative way of looking at Ratios: the output level depends on the Ratio applied once the sound crosses the Threshold.

To clarify, a 4:1 compression Ratio means that the signals exceeding the Threshold are reduced by a factor of 4, in other words, they are quartered. A 2:1 compression Ratio means that signals exceeding the Threshold are halved.

The diagram in Figure 3.2 shows compression being applied to a waveform and - assuming an input peaking at 0dB - the point to which a 2:1 and 4:1 Ratio setting would attempt to compress that waveform:

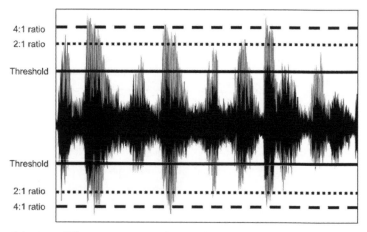

Figure 3.2: How different compression Ratios would affect a real waveform.

Now that we understand how Threshold and Ratio work, let's take a look at Attack and Release, as shown in Figure 3.3:

Figure 3.3: The Attack and Release controls on Logic Pro X's compressor.

The process of compression begins once a signal breaches the Threshold. Attack is a useful parameter that controls how quickly this occurs, giving the producer a much greater degree of leverage over the process of compression. Attack controls how long a significant proportion of the gain reduction process takes, once a signal over the Threshold has been detected.
This generally tends to be a proportion of about two thirds of the overall gain reduction duration.

Along with a control for the Attack, compressors will also offer a control for the related process of Release. Release defines how long it takes for the compressor to restore roughly two thirds of the signal, as shown in Figure 3.4:

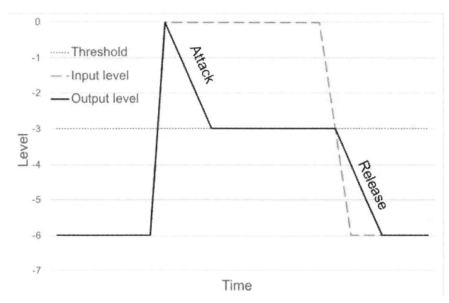

Figure 3.4: A hypothetical compression process. Notice the time it takes for the output level to reduce: this is the Attack stage. Equally, notice the time it takes for the level to be restored: this is the Release stage.

Compressors will sometimes also offer an Auto Release function, as depicted in Figure 3.5:

Figure 3.5: The Auto release button below the manual release pot in Ableton Live.

Utilising Auto Release is a great way to let the compressor 'choose' its own Release times, rather than applying a one-size-fits-all Release time, which might only work for some aspects of your sound. By monitoring the intensity levels over several simultaneous time periods, Auto Release can provide an algorithmic flexibility across compression, allowing a fast recovery time for the loudest transients (to maintain their loudness), whilst simultaneously restoring the original signal more gently after longer, slower peaks in order to smooth them out and avoid them sounding overly compressed. The downside to Auto Release is that there may be specific points in your sound where you want Release to occur — such as the compression of a kick drum, for example — and these might not match up with the ones picked by the algorithm.

Attack and Release control more than just the initial gain reduction process. Real audio signals are messy, and their intensity curve continuously varies. Even an audio signal that sounds stable to the ear, such as a telephone dial tone, bounces up and down in intensity, as shown in Figure 3.6:

Figure 3.6: The waveform of a telephone dial tone. Notice the peaks and troughs in intensity.

On this basis, when an audio signal is breaching the Threshold, a compressor will either be applying more gain reduction, or letting some of that gain reduction through, in order to meet the Ratio set by the producer. It will always be Attacking or Releasing.

You can see this on a compressor with a needle that displays gain reduction. The needle - as shown in Figure 3.7 - will always be moving between the left and the right.

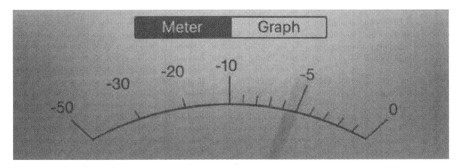

Figure 3.7: Logic Pro X's compression meter. Notice how the needle is moving; this simulates the continuously moving needles of many hardware compressors.

When the needle moves left, the amount of gain reduction is increasing, and Attack is at play. When the needle moves right, the amount of gain reduction is decreasing, and Release is at play. These two controls continuously dance with one another.

Having looked at Threshold, Ratio, Attack and Release, we now need to understand that these four parameters occupy two discrete dimensions: level and time.

The Threshold and Ratio parameters control the *level* of gain reduction applied by the compressor, whilst Attack and Release control the *timing* of how this occurs. Understanding these two dimensions is key to implementing effective compression; if you get lost when working with these parameters, just remind yourself that you're only actually changing either the level or the time.

As a reminder, Table 3.2 summarises these key controls:

Term	Definition	Dimension
Threshold	The threshold of volume at which the compressor starts working	Level
Ratio	The extent to which the signal is compressed	Level
Attack	How long the gain reduction process takes after the Threshold is breached (the attack time is roughly two thirds of the total time)	Time
Release	The speed at which the compressor releases the gain reduction process (the release time is roughly two thirds of the total time)	Time

3.2: Compressor Signal Flow

Let's now look at the basic signal flow of a compressor, as represented by Figure 3.8:

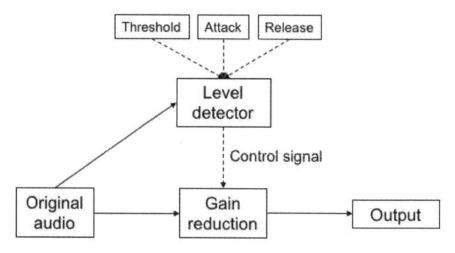

Figure 3.8: The basic signal flow of a compressor.

We can see that the original audio signal is in effect split into two signals: a primary signal that is subject to gain reduction, and a secondary signal monitored by the level detector. Once the level detector has done its work, a control signal is then issued to implement the gain reduction process and compression is applied.

3.2: Compression: Advanced Features

Whilst the four features of Attack, Release, Threshold and Ratio define the basic function of a compressor, compressors often support additional, advanced features that can greatly assist you to refine your use of this powerful music production tool. In this section we'll take a look at some of the most important ones.

3.2.1: Knee

Many compressors offer a useful function called 'Knee'. As you know, compressors apply gain reduction to sounds that breach the Threshold. Knee governs precisely *how* they approach this task. The predominant terms in knee controls are 'Hard Knee' and 'Soft Knee', although some compressors will offer the user a sliding scale of values between these two opposites.

When compressing a sound with a wide dynamic range, you might want the compressor to clamp down on sounds that significantly breach the Threshold, whilst easing off on sounds that only breach the Threshold slightly. This is where Knee controls come in.

Soft Knee compression helps you accomplish this by subtly increasing the compression Ratio directly in proportion to the intensity of the signal that exceeds the Threshold.

Hard Knee compression meanwhile, applies gain reduction at the set Ratio regardless of the extent to which the Threshold is breached, whether that is 0.2dB over the Threshold or 20dB over the Threshold. This is not an issue when the breaches are small, but at higher Ratios it can make the compression very noticeable, leading to unwanted results.

This is demonstrated by the graph in Figure 3.9:

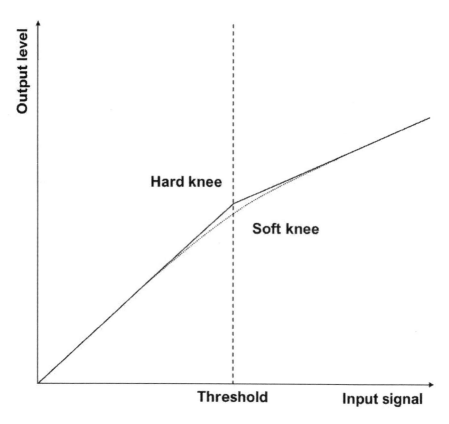

Figure 3.9: Hard knee vs soft knee. Notice the smoother transition as the input level crosses the Threshold.

As you can see, once the Threshold has been breached, Hard Knee applies the exact set Ratio required, whereas Soft Knee gradually increases the Ratio in relation to the amount by which the Threshold is breached. As you continue with your music production efforts, you will really begin to appreciate the subtle effects that can be achieved through the Knee controllers.

3.2.2: Peak vs RMS

Depending on the type of compressor you use, there may also be controls present that allow you to choose between 'Peak' and 'RMS' compression. The purpose of these controls is actually fairly straightforward, although the way they go about this can seem complex.

Peak and RMS define how the compressor goes about 'listening' for peaks above the Threshold. Whereas Peak means the compressor responds to the short peaks within a signal, RMS is more subtle. RMS stands for Root Mean Squared, which is a method of averaging the intensity of a sound over a period. RMS is therefore more tolerant of large but sudden peaks in intensity. This means that its effect is slower and softer overall, because the compressor is looking at how the average intensity of a period of sound compares to the Threshold, rather than just looking for the peaks.

Like the difference between Soft Knee and Hard Knee, it's a matter of personal preference. Peak compression at a high Ratio can sound unnatural, whereas RMS compression is far closer to the way that our ears naturally perceive sound intensity.

Some compressors also have a related 'Expand' function. Expand is rather counterintuitive; it means that instead of *reducing* the gain, it *increases* the gain, which allows you to harness Ratios under the value of 1, as depicted in Figure 3.10:

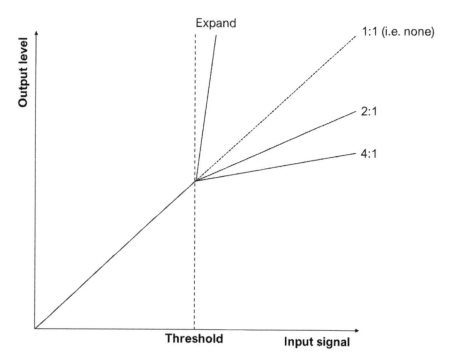

Figure 3.10: The Expand feature. Notice how once the input level breaches the Threshold, the compressor increases the gain.

This means that the compressor augments the intensity of your peaks, rather than reducing them. Since this is contrary to the traditional functions of a compressor, it is fairly rare to find Expand controls on traditional compressors.

3.2.3: Make Up Gain

Once your signal has been compressed, you need to consider what you want to do with it. If you have added a significant degree of gain reduction, your signal's peaks will have been flattened out, leaving you with lots of spare dynamic range.

This means that you can increase the overall intensity of the signal, as shown in Figure 3.11:

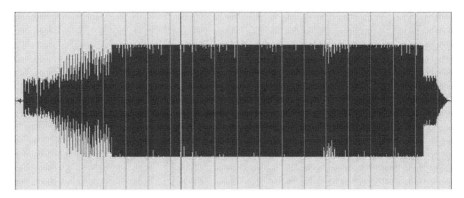

Figure 3.11: The waveform of a track where the peaks have been flattened by compression. Notice the empty space to the top and bottom of the waveform; this is spare dynamic range.

Figure 3.12 depicts the same waveform where the intensity has been increased - observe how the available dynamic range has now been filled:

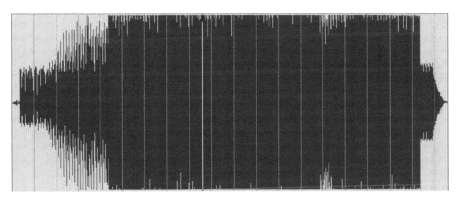

Figure 3.12: This is the same waveform as figure 3.11, but with increased gain. Compression's flattening of the peaks has allowed us to increase the overall intensity.

So why not accomplish this by simply increasing the level of the channel on the DAW's mixer? Whilst this might work in theory, it would have certain drawbacks. Make Up gain's utility is to bring the maximum intensity of your audio back to the point where it was before you compressed. Increasing the level on the DAW's mixer would mean that your gain reduction actually reduced the maximum intensity of the audio, leaving you with far less wiggle room when mixing your channels together. Rather than running this risk, the optimum way to increase the overall intensity of the signal is to increase the gain within the compressor's output. This is why it is known as 'Make Up gain' - because you're making up for the intensity you've removed from the peaks.

Figure 3.13 shows the range of possible Make Up gain values in Logic Pro X's compressor:

Figure 3.13: The Make Up gain pot on Logic Pro X's compressor.

Many modern compressors offer Auto Gain. This means that instead of applying your own Make Up gain and then having to work out which Make Up level you want, the compressor will do the work for you. In Logic Pro X's compressor, for example, you can set the compressor a target, as shown in Figure 3.14:

Figure 3.14: Logic Pro X's compressor's Auto Gain options. You can set it a target of 0dB, -12dB, or turn Auto Gain off altogether.

The compressor will then increase the output intensity of the sound to the level you've chosen. This means that you only need to think about the gain reduction process, rather than trying to compensate for the gain reduction you've applied.

3.2.4: Limiter

You might have heard of a device called a Limiter. A Limiter is essentially a compressor that prevents all signals above the Threshold from being breached. In other words, it functions as a brick wall, a 'You-Shall-Not-Pass' compressor. Because of this, many compressors can also function well as Limiters.

Figure 3.15 shows the process of limiting once a signal crosses the Threshold:

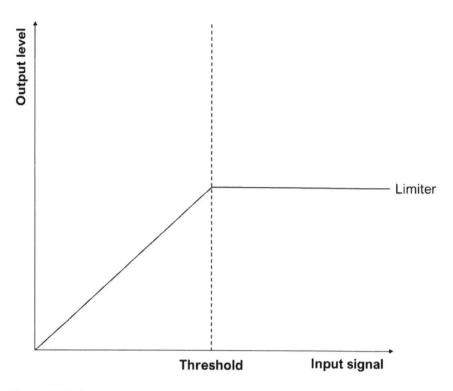

Figure 3.15: The relationship between the input and output levels on a Limiter. Notice how once the input level reaches the Threshold, infinite gain reduction is applied to ensure it is not breached.

Both compressors and Limiters achieve limiting by applying an inf:1 (infinite to 1) Ratio above the Threshold.

Some digital compressors allow for a Limiter to be applied to the compressor's output, for example in Logic Pro X's compressor, which offers the benefit of being able to limit an already-compressed signal. This is shown in Figure 3.16:

Figure 3.16: The Limiter function within Logic Pro X's compressor. Notice the on/off switch—this is because the Ratio of a Limiter is a constant inf:1.

Alternatively, a Limiter may be offered as a standalone effects unit in its own right. Ableton Live is a good example of a program that provides this, as shown in Figure 3.17:

Figure 3.17: Ableton Live's standalone Limiter. This contains some features you are not yet familiar with, however the function is the same as in Logic Pro X's version.

3.2.5: Lookahead

First appearing as a commercial proposition on digital compressors during the early 1990s, Lookahead is now a common feature to be found on many modern compressors.

Imagine a scenario like the one illustrated in Figure 3.18 below, where the sound you're attempting to compress is immediate. It does not build in intensity and you have no indication it is coming:

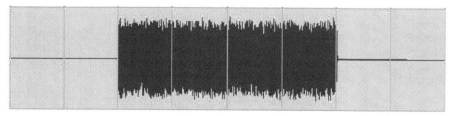

Figure 3.18: A waveform with an immediate attack. Notice how it starts sounding with no warning.

This lack of warning caused issues on older compressors; unable to see into the future, the compression would usually kick in too late, causing the awkward peak shown in Figure 3.19:

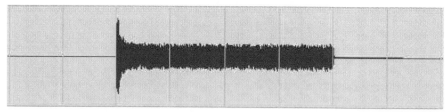

Figure 3.19: Notice the slow gain reduction caused by the compressor responding to the peak in intensity after it has occurred.

Modern compressors however, have a function to fix this, called Lookahead.

Lookahead essentially reviews the incoming signal to compress the peaks just as they enter the circuitry, so that the signal is compressed perfectly, as shown in Figure 3.20:

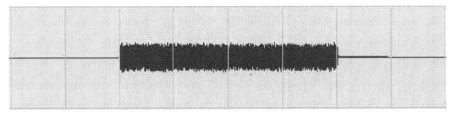

Figure 3.20: The same signal with the Lookahead function applied. Notice the awkward peak at the beginning of the signal has disappeared. The Lookahead function has given the compressor the 'foresight' to anticipate the peak in intensity.

The method by which this is achieved is simple. In hardware compressors, the compressor delays its output by a few milliseconds. This is long enough for the compressor to be able to analyse the signal, but not so long that it will have a noticeable impact on the track.

Software compressors meanwhile employ various different approaches to accomplish this objective. Often this involves the compressor reading the realtime signal, whilst outputting a duplicate that has been delayed by a few milliseconds. This duplicate will then have the compressor's reactions to the peaks already in place. Whilst this slowing of the track is so minor that it should be unnoticeable, most modern DAWs can correct any resulting latency issues via an automated delay compensation function.

Lookahead is not offered as a function on all DAW compressors. Logic's compressor, for example, doesn't bother with Lookahead, and instead offers a 0ms Attack - which performs much the same task - as you can see in Figure 3.21:

Figure 3.21: Logic Pro X's compressor's Attack dial. Notice the 0ms setting; this would be impossible on analog compressors.

Ableton's compressor offers 1ms and 10ms Lookahead, while 0ms Lookahead is enabled by default, as depicted in Figure 3.22:

Figure 3.22: Ableton Live's Lookahead drop-down, offering no Lookahead (0ms) as well as 1ms and 10ms Lookahead options.

Ableton's Lookahead can be very helpful when you're compressing a live signal coming in externally. When playing off the sequencer itself, however, Ableton's Lookahead doesn't really perform any useful function.

3.2.6: Sidechain

Sidechain is a feature now found in most modern compressors. Used correctly, it will transform your music production. Later on in this book we'll delve more deeply into how to make use of Sidechain to best advantage, but for now let's explore its basic functionality.

You will already be familiar with Sidechain from radio broadcasts, where it was first employed to allow the voice of the DJ to be heard alongside the music. The signal of the DJ's voice would automatically trigger a compressor to reduce the intensity of the background music being played.

It wasn't long however before music producers realised the exciting potential of Sidechain as a technique to enliven a sound. Used since the 1960s, Sidechain is now heard most prominently in electronic music. If you listen to the first minute of *I Remember* by deadmau5, for example, you can hear how the synthesizers seem to bounce and breathe in rhythm with the drums. Whilst there are several effects being used here, Sidechain is the one giving the production that powerful, bouncy energy.

Sidechain is where the compressor is triggered into action through use of an external signal. This will have an effect on all instruments whose signals are routed through the compressor. This means that rather than calculating whether the input signal has met the Threshold, the compressor instead calculates whether a different, external signal has met the Threshold, as shown in Figure 3.23:

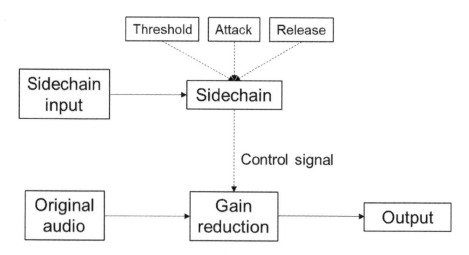

Figure 3.23: The signal path of a compressor using Sidechain.

Imagine an input signal 6dB above the Threshold, but a sidechain input level only 3dB above the Threshold, as shown in Figure 3.24:

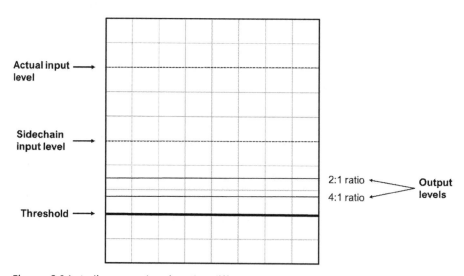

Figure 3.24: A diagram showing the different output levels of different Ratios applied to a sidechained signal.

As you can see in Figure 3.24, even though the input level is 6dB above the Threshold, a 2:1 Ratio compresses the sound to 1.5dB over the Threshold. This is because the compressor is analysing the sidechain input level of 3dB above the Threshold.

If you haven't used Sidechain before, it may appear to be an additional and unnecessary layer of confusion when calculating the effect of your Threshold and Ratio. However, the implications of Sidechain for music production are immense.

To provide an example, Figure 3.25 depicts the waveform of a pad with no compression applied:

Figure 3.25: The waveform of a pad with no compression applied.

Figure 3.26 depicts the waveform of a kick drum:

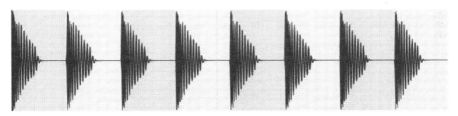

Figure 3.26: The waveform of a kick drum.

If the pad is routed to a compressor however and the kick drum is used as the Sidechain source, the 'bounce' of the kick drum makes an impression upon the pad levels, as can be seen in Figure 3.27:

Figure 3.27: The waveform of the pad in figure 3.26 when a kick drum is used as a 'Sidechain' on the pad. Notice now the levels of the pad seem to 'bounce' up and down in time with the kick.

This can be further observed on the compressor's display, as shown in Figure 3.28:

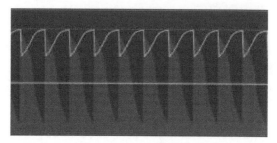

Figure 3.28: Sidechain compression in Ableton Live 10's compressor. Notice how the regular beat of the kick drum causes 'waves' in on the compressor's display.

Another interesting aspect of Sidechain is that it doesn't require the source to be audible on the main Output. This means that a producer can Sidechain a rhythm source into a compressor to add a rhythmic bounce to a sound, even though that rhythm source can't be heard on the main output. Equally, the source can be made audible, so that the levels of a guitar drop slightly when a vocalist sings, for example. When used appropriately, this technique can bring your music production to life.

Some compressors additionally offer Sidechain EQ, or Sidechain Filter. This can be used to remove unwanted frequencies from the sidechain source. Imagine, for example, a live mix where you want to use Sidechain to balance a rhythm guitar sitting mostly in the upper register, with the upper register of the drum track. A lot of lower-register information such as the kick, toms and lower end of the snare will create transients, causing the compressor to apply gain reduction at the wrong time, and the compression of the rhythm guitar will suffer accordingly. This is where Sidechain EQ or Filter comes in, because it will allow you to select which bands of your Sidechain source to use. This frees you to synchronise your compression with particular frequencies of the Sidechain input signal.

Figure 3.29 shows Ableton Live's Sidechain EQ. In this example it has been set to filter frequencies under 2.2 kHz from the Sidechain source, before it arrives at the compressor:

Figure 3.29: Ableton's Sidechain EQ function.

Sidechain EQ can strongly affect the gain reduction caused by Sidechain, so use it with caution. If you're ever unsure, use the

Listen button (the headphones icon in the image above) to monitor the signal coming into your compressor with greater accuracy.

Sidechain is an exceptionally useful function. Once you've had time to explore and master it in full, you will come to appreciate the enormous implications it holds for your music production.

3.2.7: Wet/Dry/Depth

As shown in Figure 3.30, Wet/Dry, sometimes known as Depth, is a function more commonly found on effects units such as delays or flangers:

Figure 3.30: The Dry/Wet pot found on many of Ableton Live's effects units.

It allows you to select the proportion of the original signal you wish the effects unit to act upon. 100% Wet is the entire compressed signal, 50% Wet is a 50/50 mix of the compressed and uncompressed signals and 0% Wet means none of the compressed signal comes through the output; in other words there is no compression at all.

Figure 3.31 shows this relationship:

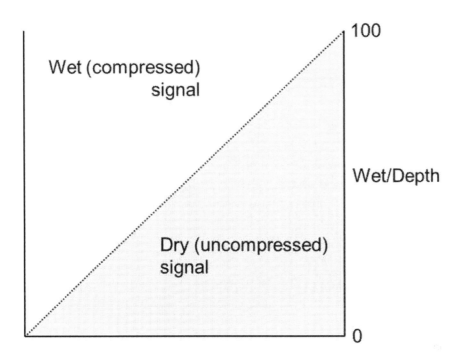

100

Wet (compressed) signal

Wet/Depth

Dry (uncompressed) signal

0

Figure 3.31: A diagram showing how much of each signal you let through using the Wet/Dry pot.

The Wet/Dry function is helpful for those times when you have your Ratio, Threshold and Knee perfect, but you can hear that the signal is a tad too compressed. In this scenario, you can use Wet/Dry to dial back the compression without having to reconfigure your most important settings.

3.2.8: Saturation/Distortion

We have already mentioned the 'character' that vintage hardware compressors add to a sound. Saturation and / or Distortion are an effect that is normally found on standalone distortion plugins. It has also begun appearing modern digital compressors however, and it allows you to imitate some of this traditional hardware character.

The Saturation/Distortion function achieves this by artificially overloading the signal path, creating warm, harmonic-rich 'fuzz', similar to how distortion on guitar amplifiers overloads the signal path.

Figure 3.32 depicts the Distortion pot in Logic Pro X's compressor:

Figure 3.32: The Distortion pot on Logic Pro X's compressor.

It could be argued that bolted-on Saturation is a superfluous feature, since it does nothing to compress the signal. If you wanted to saturate your signal, you could simply do so using a specialist plugin. It must be said though, that the results of this function on some digital compressors tend to sound positive, especially when sounds are in need of some grit, like lead synthesizers. It can give sawtooth chords extra scream and rhodes an added layer of fuzz. Used with discretion, Saturation/Distortion is a useful tool for adding small amounts of depth and warmth to your instruments.

3.2.9: Range

Range provides a way to reduce the overall degree of gain reduction that a compressor can apply. It is set in dB and acts as a 'cap', preventing a compressor from applying any more gain reduction than the Range allows.

A large Range - of 60dB, for example - would essentially have no effect, if only because it would be extremely rare for a compressor to apply 60dB of gain reduction. 4dB of Range however would have an enormous effect, because it would constrain the compressor to a maximum of 4dB of gain reduction, as you can see in Figure 3.33:

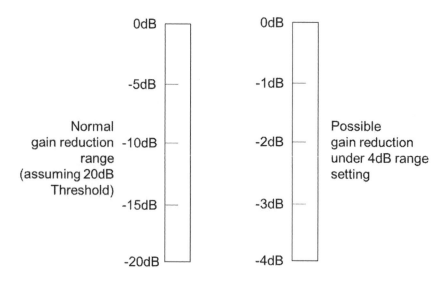

Figure 3.33: Possible gain reduction under different Range configurations.

This function can be helpful when you are looking to restrain a sound subtly, but still allow it to express its dynamic range.

Range is a handy, but by no means vital feature. A similar degree of restraint can be accomplished using a high Threshold. Range only becomes truly useful when you require absolute precision.

This concludes our exploration of the main features found on a compressor. In the next Chapter we will begin learning how to harness the power of compression in an easy, systematic manner.

Summary

To conclude this Chapter, Table 3.3 provides a convenient list of advanced functions.

Table 3.3: A summary of all the functions we've explored in this Chapter.

Term	Definition
Hard Knee	Any sound breaching the threshold has gain reduction applied at the given ratio.
Soft Knee	The compressor applies harder gain reduction according to the extent of the breach of the threshold.
RMS	Root Mean Squared – a way of measuring the average of the waveform over a period. A more subtle form of compression.
Peak	Measurement of the Peak volume – a fast-acting, reactive form of compression.
Make-up	Amplification of the compressed signal to compensate for overall gain reduction.
Limiter	A compressor where no signal can breach the Threshold, essentially an infinite ratio.
Lookahead	Delaying the input signal so that the compressor can 'foresee' peaks in volume.
Sidechain	The use of an external signal to trigger gain reduction.
Sidechain EQ	The filtering of the external sidechain signal, to remove undesired peaks.
Wet/Dry/Depth	The mix between the original signal and the compressed signal.
Saturation/Distortion	The artificial distortion of the signal to create desirable harmonics.
Range	The constraint of the range of possible gain reduction.

Chapter 4: Learning Compression

4.1: Objectivity

In comparison with effects such as Reverb, Delay or even EQ, the changes you make using compression can be difficult to discern, making it harder to know whether you are doing the right thing. This makes learning to use compression by trial and error more challenging. It is consequently important to maintain your objectivity. You will need to be cold, rational, and scientific when applying compression, else you run the risk of thinking you're improving your track when you're actually making it sound worse.

There are several ways you can do this. If you make these practices into a habit, compression will become easier and more comfortable and your music production skills will steadily increase as a result.

1. Use the Bypass function. If you are not familiar with Bypass, it is one of the most important features on any effects unit. It allows you to switch the unit off, passing the signal through it unaltered. This allows you to make a quick comparison of your sound, both with and without the effect. To Bypass an effects unit in Ableton, click the Power button in the top left:

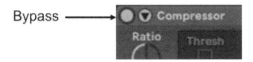

Bypass

Figure 4.1: The Bypass button in Ableton.

When Bypassed, the controls of the effects unit will grey out, indicating that the effect is now Bypassed.

Compare the left and right-hand sides of Figure 4.2:

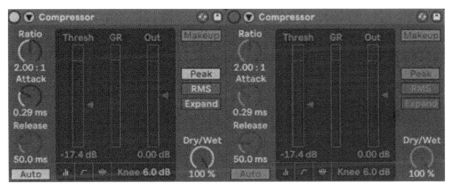

Figure 4.2: A side-by-side comparison of Ableton's compressor. On the left, the compressor is active. On the right, the compressor is bypassed.

Whenever you are compressing, regularly Bypass the compression and listen carefully to the difference the compressor is making. Regular comparison of the compressed sound with the original will allow you to spot when you're getting carried away and adding too much compression, or actually wasting effort by making very little noticeable difference to the overall sound.

2. Use Make Up gain to ensure that the peak level of your original, uncompressed sound matches the peak level of your sound after compression. In music, 'louder' often sounds 'better'. Have you ever been blown away by a piece of music in a club, only

to find it dull to listen to at home? It is easy to convince yourself that you have made a track sound bigger and warmer, when all you've done is increase the volume.

Once you have compressed, your resulting input and output volumes should be as close to the same as possible. To check this, measure your peak volume using the mixer in your DAW with compression Bypassed, and then measure it again with your compression active:

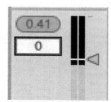

Figure 4.3: The peak measurement meter in Ableton, in this case displaying a value of +0.41dB.

Apply the difference between your compressed and uncompressed volumes to the Output intensity of your compressor. If your peak volume was -1dB before compression and +2dB afterwards for example, reduce the Output volume by 3dB, as shown here in Figure 4.4:

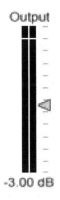

Figure 4.4: The mixer's intensity reduced by 3dB.

By doing this you won't fool yourself into thinking you're a compression wizard, when all you're actually doing is smashing the intensity upwards.

3. Learn to listen to the music that you write in a new and different way. As a musician, you're naturally inspired by great music. If you're writing your own music, you'll be writing in terms of your own emotion. Because of this, you may be used to listening out for timbre and melody, both of which are highly emotive content. Compression requires you to listen less like a musician, and more like a scientist. You will need to attune your ears specifically to the dynamic range. This will take time and experience, but as a starting point, listen out for:

- The aggressiveness of the transients in your sounds, especially drum sounds. Do they sound sharper because of what you're doing, or is your compression making them sound blunt?

- The pressure of the sound. Does the sound inhale and exhale over time, or does it have a constant, unvarying pressure?

- The tone of the sound. Is it becoming distorted or warped?

- The ambience of the sound, including any 'pumping' or movement. If it pumps, does it do so in sync with your music?

- The dynamic range. All music has loud points and quiet points, but do yours sound like they're in the right place?

Analysing your music in this way requires the use of both of the techniques previously mentioned. You should be using Bypass to make comparisons according to the above criteria, and you will need to ensure that your pre and post-compression volumes are matched, in order to be certain you're not giving yourself false information by artificially boosting the volume.

4. Start with Soft Knee *on* and any Saturation *off*. You can switch to Hard Knee later if you want further control, but Soft Knee will give you the most natural feel, which will help you gain better results faster. Saturation, meanwhile, will give you artificial distortion. This can sound good at first, but it will eventually hold you back by preventing you from evaluating the core parameters of your compression in a systematic manner.

5. Make full use of visualisations offered. Most modern computerised plugins will provide several ways to visualise the gain reduction being applied. These are often gain reduction meters, which fill downwards as gain reduction is applied, as seen in Figure 4.5:

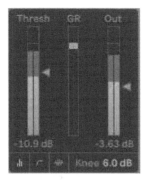

Figure 4.5: Ableton's compression meters. The GR column in the centre shows the amount of gain reduction being applied.

Another common visualisation is the Transfer Curve, as depicted in Figure 4.6, with input shown horizontally and output shown vertically:

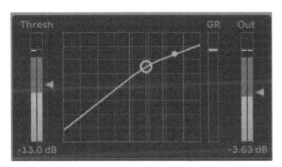

Figure 4.6: Ableton's Transfer Curve display, showing the relationship between the input and output levels.

A popular alternative to these is the Activity View, as shown in Figure 4.7, which shows the input level, gain reduction and Threshold as a chart, allowing you to judge the relationship between the three factors:

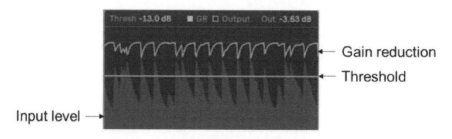

Thresh -13.0 dB   ■ GR □ Output   Out -3.63 dB

Gain reduction

Threshold

Input level →

Figure 4.7: Ableton's Activity View, showing the input level, degree of gain reduction and Threshold over time, allowing you to make objective adjustments.

Implemented correctly, the tips in this section will have you well on your way to being a compression scientist.

4.2: A systematic approach

When you are learning to use compression, you need to take a methodical approach to it. In this section, we will look at three such systematic approaches. Which one you follow is up to you, but we'll compare and summarise them at the end to help you choose between them.

4.2.1: Method One: the Top-Down System

Top-down compression is one of the easiest systems when you are starting out. The logic behind this method is that the effect of the Attack and Release settings can initially be difficult to discern. This system therefore involves applying extreme compression in order to highlight the effect of the Attack and Release settings.

This is how to go about it:

1.   Add the compressor to the signal.

2. Calculate the peak level of the uncompressed signal using the peak level monitor on the DAW's mixer, as shown in Figure 4.8 (you can guesstimate if you are using a hardware mixer):

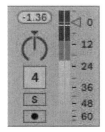

Figure 4.8: The figure above the pan pot is your peak level.

3. Set your Threshold to around 25dB below that peak level, as depicted in Figure 4.9.

Figure 4.9: A Threshold set roughly 25dB below the peak level. The peak level in Figure 4.8 is roughly -1dB, so the Threshold has been set at -26dbB.

4. Set your Ratio to inf:1, applying limiting compression, as shown in Figure 4.10:

Figure 4.10: The Ratio set to inf:1, applying total, limiting compression.

5. Use Attack and Release to choose which peaks you want to allow through, using Activity View if it's available to you.

Figure 4.11 shows an Attack of 0.01ms. This means that the applied gain reduction mirrors the peaks and troughs of the underlying audio:

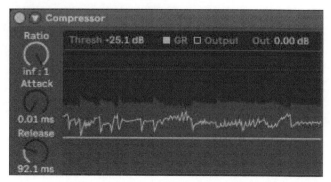

Figure 4.11: The gain reduction at 0.01ms Attack mirrors the peaks and troughs of the intensity of the underlying audio.

By way of contrast, Figure 4.12 shows that when the Attack is set 40ms, the compressor is more selective as to where it applies gain reduction:

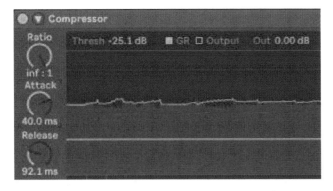

Figure 4.12: The gain reduction at 40ms Attack is more selective, clamping down more slowly on major peaks.

Use Attack and Release in conjunction with Bypass and the listening techniques we've previously discussed, to arrive at a sound that complements your audio's rhythmic character. What you'll now have is a highly exaggerated version of the gain reduction timing you will actually implement.

6. Bring the Ratio to 8:1 or so, creating severe, but not extreme compression.

7. Bring the Threshold up by around 10dB. You will notice that the compression sounds less extreme now, but the rhythmic timing of it still sounds good.

8. Bring the Ratio to a point below 8:1 that you are comfortable with—such as 4:1 for example - then continue adjusting the Threshold and Ratio to the stage where you feel the dynamics are right. It is at this point that you can resume Bypassing the compressor to assess the effect it's having on your signal.

As you have likely surmised, the purpose of the top-down approach is to highlight the effect of your Attack and Release settings by exaggerating their effect. It is an aggressive approach.

Once you have mastered the top-down method, you can begin to use compression in a more subtle manner. This requires the bottom-up method.

4.2.2: Method Two: the Bottom-Up System

1. Add your compressor to the track you want to compress.

2. Set it to a 1:1 Ratio and 0dB Threshold. This essentially bypasses the compressor.

3. Slowly increase the Ratio and decrease the Threshold until you have achieved your required degree of compression, but completely ignore the timing.

4. Finally, change first the Attack and then the Release, to produce the dynamics you require - whether this is a sharp dynamic using low Attack and Release, a softer dynamic using high Attack and Release or some combination of the two. It is at this point that you should use Bypass to evaluate the effect of your compression.

The advantage of the bottom-up method is that you can work on the most important aspect of compression - your dynamics - confident that the timing adjustments can be left until last.

4.2.3: Method Three: The Templated System

There is a great deal of information readily available regarding the best way to compress particular instruments, much of which can be very useful when working with conventional mixes in traditional genres. For this reason, the templated method is one of the easiest to follow since it offers you a pre-made foundation that can be adapted to meet your own particular requirements.

To follow the templated system, use the dynamic properties of your instrument to look up an instrument with similar properties in the following table and adopt this as a starting point from which to develop your own compression. A lead synth possesses similar dynamics to an electric guitar for example, and a pad has similar dynamics to strings, so you can use the configurations in Table 4.1 as your basis and work outward from there:

Sound	Attack	Release	Ratio
Vocals	10-100ms	500ms-1s	2:1-4:1
Electric guitar	20-50ms	1-2s	4:1-inf:1
Acoustic guitar	100-400ms	100-400ms	2:1-4:1
Strings	40-50ms	100-200ms	2:1-3:1
Drums	10-50ms	10-50ms	2:1-4:1
Piano	100-300ms	50-300ms	2:1-4:1
Bass	15-50ms	100-300ms	4:1

Table 4.1: A table of traditional compression configurations for different instruments.

These templates can help you to understand what compression should sound customarily sound like for particular instruments, but applying compression prescriptively can only get you so far. By using the top-down and then the bottom-up method, you will find that you begin building your own subconscious model of compression that will serve you well in the long run, opening you up to a new world of creative possibility.

It is also the case that if you are working in a non-traditional genre - such as cutting-edge EDM, for example - taking an open and creative approach to compression may give you far better results. Some of the best producers in the world got to where they did by departing from orthodox approaches.

I strongly recommend that you practise applying compression to a variety of different instruments within your DAW before moving onto the next Chapter. If you are new to compression, begin with the templated and top-down and methods. If you are more experienced, use all three methods.

Try applying compression to five instruments that have very different dynamics and sounds to one another, for example:

- A lead guitar.
- A spoken word vocal.
- An EDM lead.
- A live drum recording.
- An electronic drum machine.

If you struggle to find samples for all five, websites such as www.freesound.org have a library of free downloadable samples that you can use.

A summary of the three methods discussed in this Chapter is shown in Table 4.2:

Table 4.2: A summary of the compression systems previously discussed in this Chapter.

Method	Summary	Benefit
Top-down	Work on Attack and Release first using harsh compression	Emphasises Attack and Release, which can be difficult to discern if you're new to compression
Bottom-up	Work on Ratio and Threshold first	Allows you to configure the dynamics if you already intuitively understand what timing you will use
Templated	Use a template as a starting point	Quick and easy results

Chapter 5: Advanced Compression Techniques

In addition to the basic techniques already outlined, there are more advanced techniques that have produced great results for music producers over the years. These tried-and-tested methods display the remarkable ingenuity of the producers and engineers who pioneered them. This Chapter will introduce you to three of the most exciting.

Audio examples of all three techniques discussed in this Chapter are freely available for download at: https://compression.producers.guide. You can use these examples to compare how they sound before and after compression has been applied. You can also experiment on them yourself if you wish.

5.1: Parallel Compression

In the late 1970s, *Studio Sound* magazine carried an article detailing an exciting technique of compression called parallel compression, also known as New York compression. It was primarily designed for classical recordings, but music producers soon spotted its potential for application across a far broader musical context.

The crux of the technique involved mixing a dry (uncompressed) signal with a heavily compressed wet version. This served to attenuate the peaks significantly, allowing a high degree of Make Up gain whilst retaining some natural dynamic range.

So, how would you go about employing parallel compression in your own music?

A good starting point would be to set your compressor to 100% Wet and then configure your compressor for harsh compression. The following settings, as shown in Figure 5.1, show how this might look in practice:

- -30-40dB Threshold.
- Ratio between 5:1 and 20:1.
- Instant Attack.
- Fast Release, between 50ms and 100ms.
- Make Up gain to bring the signal up to the input level.

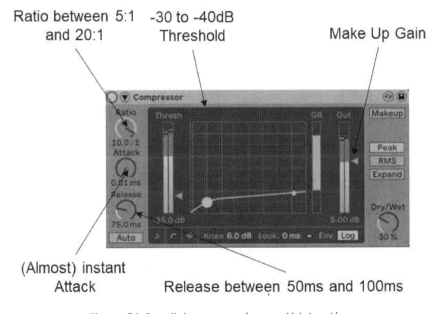

Figure 5.1: Parallel compression on Ableton Live.

When you first audition this effect, you should hear a drastic amount of compression on your track. Now, move the Wet/Dry back to 100% Dry and slowly increase the amount of wet signal, listening for something that sounds sharp and full, whilst still retaining its basic naturalness. Don't worry too much about the technical details for now; just let your ear guide you, listening out for the desirable features outlined in Chapter 4.

The reason that parallel compression works so well is that a very low Threshold combined with a high Ratio aggressively compresses the sound's dynamic range. This means that you can apply a substantial degree of Make Up gain, bringing the softest sounds up to an audible level and emphasising the fine details.

The remarkable ability of parallel compression to highlight the details in a subtle and controlled manner is the very aspect that made it so suitable for classical music recordings. A light harp sound for example would be completely overwhelmed by a full-blown orchestral tutti (a section where all the instruments play together). Of course, it would make no sense for the harp sound to have the same intensity as the orchestral tutti, and this is where parallel compression came in so useful. The Wet/Dry function gave the producer a much greater degree of control over the representation of dynamic range, allowing the delicate harp to be suitably positioned within the sonic context; loud enough to be heard, but not unnaturally so.

Depending on the Wet/Dry settings used, parallel compression offers the producer the potential to bring instruments with a large dynamic range – such as vocals, piano or acoustic guitar tracks, for example - under full control.

5.2: Bus Compression

Bus compression, also known as Mix bus compression, is a high-risk, high-reward compression technique used to glue together the individual elements of a mix. When using bus compression however, there is a big twist: it is put on your Master Output. This means that every single element of your mix will be routed through it. If you get it right, the result will be a warmer, more cohesive and exciting musical texture. Be that as it may, this is not a technique to be undertaken lightly, and it would be wise to obtain a strong grounding in music production before you attempt it.

The point at which bus compression should be applied is *after* you've recorded all the layers of your intended mix, but *before* you start any serious mixing.

This is because the aim of Mix bus compression is to blend the tracks together *as they arrive* into the mix. To apply bus compression after you have mixed will force you to restart the mixing process, as you'll then be working with a different dynamic range.

As a starting point, look to compress very conservatively, as shown in Figure 5.2:

- -7dB to 10dB Threshold.
- 2:1-3:1 Ratio.
- Slow Attack time (around 100-150ms).
- Automatic Make Up switched off.
- Fast Release time (5-10ms).

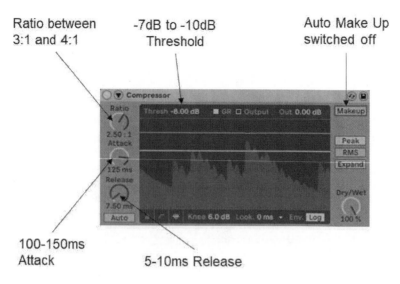

Ratio between 3:1 and 4:1

-7dB to -10dB Threshold

Auto Make Up switched off

100-150ms Attack

5-10ms Release

Figure 5.2: Bus compression on Ableton Live's compressor.

The next step is to decrease the Attack until you hear the higher elements of your track start to lose their sparkle. Set your Attack to just above the level at which that sparkle is lost.

Now increase the Release to synchronise with your track. You do this by ear, listening for when the compression starts to lightly 'pump' in time with your music. A helpful tip for synchronising your Release is to pay attention to any strong rhythmic elements such as your kick and snare. Watch the levels of Gain reduction on the compressor to ensure that the Gain reduction returns to 0 after each hit. This will ensure some degree of rhythmic synchrony.

Once you've established your Attack and Release times, bring down your Ratio and increase your Threshold, aiming for between 1dB and 2dB of overall Gain reduction. The sound should be thicker and more cohesive, but you should no longer notice much 'pump'.

Be careful not to add too much Gain reduction, as this 'pumping' will be audible on your track; it won't sit well in a mix or album and will give your mastering engineer unresolvable problems. Remember that subtlety is key to this type of compression.

Whilst applying bus compression to your Master Output is inherently risky, the good news is that you can also apply the technique on a smaller scale. For example, you could try bus compression on your drum track. To do this, route all of your drum tracks to a single bus, and then apply bus compression to it. Alternatively, you could try it on your vocal layers. Once you can hear it in action, there will be no looking back. You will confidently apply it to your entire mix.

5.3: Serial Compression

Serial compression is a fairly quirky technique, but one that can be helpful when you're struggling to produce the particular sound that you want. Put simply, serial compression makes use of more than one compressor, one after another, along the same signal path.

The main reason for doing this is to combine two distinct compression characteristics. You might wish to warm up a track using slow optical compression for instance, whilst still tightly controlling its dynamic range, using digital compression. Another example could be an otherwise good-quality drum recording that lacks something in presence, character, and drive.

You could choose to add an optical compressor, as shown in Figure 5.3:

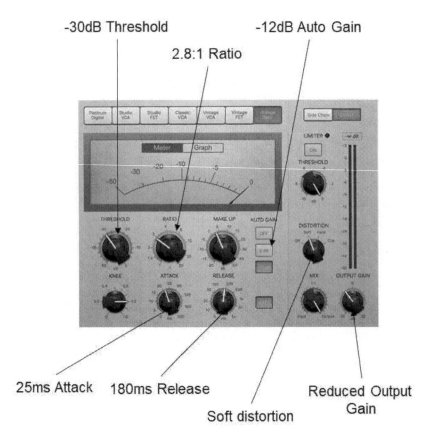

-30dB Threshold   -12dB Auto Gain

2.8:1 Ratio

25ms Attack   180ms Release   Reduced Output
                                                              Gain
                      Soft distortion

Figure 5.3: The first part of a serial compression chain on Logic Pro X.

Wanting to add the optical compressor's warmth to your drum sound, you would probably aim for aggressive, warming compression, but at a nice, slow speed. The following parameters would work well for this:

- -30dB Threshold.
- 2.8:1 Ratio.
- 25ms Attack.
- 180ms Release.
- Auto Gain.
- Soft Distortion.

- Reduced Output Gain so that the input volume matches the output volume.

The result is a much fuller, warmer, and more colourful sound. Even though your Gain meters will show that its peak volume has not changed, the drum track will also sound a lot louder, which will make it easier to place into a mix in the future.

There is one problem, however. Some of your drum sounds, particularly the snare drum, may have become rather smeared by the harsh compression, and they now lack clarity. The solution is to add a precise digital compressor before the optical compressor, as shown in Figure 5.4. This is to add additional energy to the drums, to compensate for the dampening of the optical compressor.

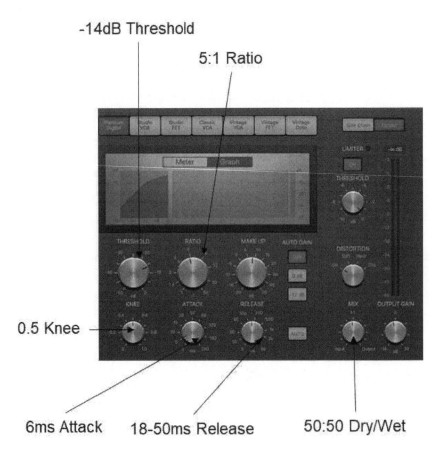

-14dB Threshold

5:1 Ratio

0.5 Knee

6ms Attack   18-50ms Release   50:50 Dry/Wet

Figure 5.4: The second part of a serial compression chain on Logic Pro X.

In this situation, the following settings can provide a good option:

- A moderate Threshold (around -14dB) to ensure that the compressor mostly acts on the peaks of the sound.
- A harsh 5:1 Ratio.
- A moderate Knee.
- A fast Attack (6ms).
- A medium Release (150ms).

If you're eagle-eyed, you will have noticed the 50/50 mix between input and output. This is because parallel compression has been applied to it, in order to retain the natural sound of the original drum track whilst adding energy via compression; 100% wet, when combined with the optical compressor, can make the drums sound a tad artificial.

Other pairings of serial compressors you could use are:

- Two digital compressors, one fast-acting to control the harshest peaks, and another slow-acting to provide further Make Up gain.

- A parallel compressor to bring up the details of a track, combined with a vintage optical compressor to add warmth.

As with bus compression, it is easy to get serial compression wrong. Achieving the correct settings on a single compressor can be a struggle; this difficulty is compounded when working with two compressors in series. Once you are comfortable with serial compression, however, the technique can open up all kinds of new opportunities to tweak sounds to your precise requirement.

Table 5.1 provides a brief summary of the three advanced compression techniques discussed in this Chapter:

Table 5.1: A summary of the advanced compression techniques discussed in this Chapter.

Compression type	Outline of method	Purpose
Parallel	Mixing extremely harsh compression with the uncompressed signal.	Highlight details in sounds with a large dynamic range.
Bus	A compressor on the main output, compressing the entire mix.	Glue together the elements of the mix.
Serial compression	Multiple compressors chained together.	Achieve multiple compression goals (e.g. warmth and dynamics) in one compression chain.

Chapter 6: Multiband Compression

Whilst ordinary compression will be sufficient to meet the needs of the majority of your music production requirements, there will nonetheless be occasions when you will require a far more precise, refined degree of control over the compression process. This is where Multiband compression comes into play.

As a music producer, you will already be familiar with multiband graphic equalisation effects. Multiband compression works in a very similar way. Picture the audible frequency range of 20 Hz to 20 kHz. Now imagine slicing that audible frequency range into several sections — ordinarily three or four, as shown in Figure 6.1:

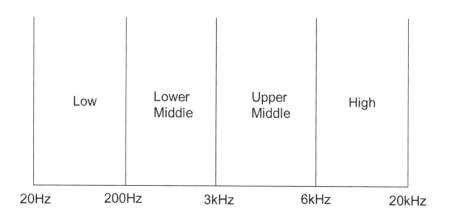

| Low | Lower Middle | Upper Middle | High |

20Hz   200Hz   3kHz   6kHz   20kHz

Figure 6.1: The audible frequency range sliced into four sections: Low, Lower Middle, Upper Middle and High.

The location of these bands on the frequency range is controlled by *crossovers*. Crossovers are the point at which the sound crosses from one frequency band into the next. In the example shown above, the crossover point between the Low and Lower Middle bands is 200Hz and the crossover point between the Lower Middle and Upper Middle bands is 3 kHz. These crossover points are adjustable, meaning you can choose which frequencies sit in within a particular band. An example of this is shown in Figure 6.2. You can see that the crossover point between the Low and Lower Middle bands is now 100Hz, whilst the crossover point between the Lower Middle and Upper Middle bands is now 2 kHz.

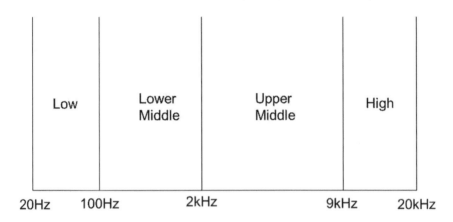

Figure 6.2: The same diagram as in figure 6.1, except the location of the crossovers has been adjusted.

Imagine that each of these bands has its own compressor, as shown in Figure 6.3 using Logic's Multiband compressor:

Individual frequency bands

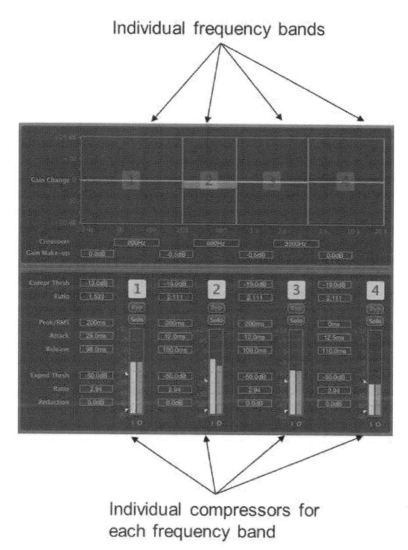

Individual compressors for each frequency band

Figure 6.3: Logic's Multiband compressor.

Multiband compression is useful when working with a sound that has a wide frequency range - usually one that you would place front and centre of your mix. If you were working with an acoustic guitar recording for example, you could use a four-band

Multiband compressor to achieve the following improvements in your sound:

1. Warm up the bottom end of the recording.
2. Tighten the dynamic range of the lower mid range.
3. Allow the upper-mid range to remain expressive.
4. Increase the volume of the high-frequency harmonics when they appear, but prevent them from lingering for too long in the recording.

This process is depicted in Figure 6.4:

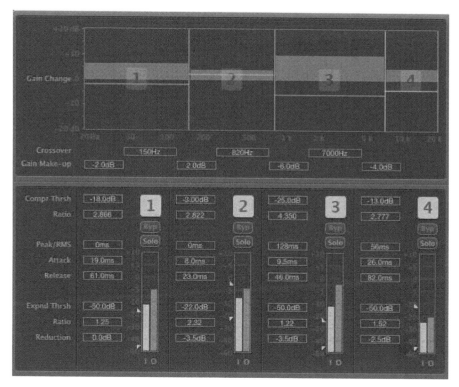

Figure 6.4: Logic's multiband compressor accomplishing several individual goals.

As you can see, it is possible to control all the parameters that you would expect on an individual compressor on each one of the four compressors. The difference is that you can now apply an individual setting to each of the four frequencies.

Multiband compressors are fairly common in DAW packages. FL Studio and Cubase have a three-band Multiband compressor, whilst Ableton and Studio One offer Multiband Dynamics. However, if your DAW software lacks a Multiband compressor, you could consider a paid plugin, such as FabFilter Pro-MB.

As you can see, Multiband compression is a convenient and useful addition to the music producer's effects toolkit. It's a complex beast however, and requires a lot of time outlay to get it just right. This means that it's often not worth using it for simple sounds.

Personally, I'd only recommend its use on sounds that span a wide frequency range, are rich in harmonic partials and have several regions of spectral interest across the frequency range, such as pianos, vocals or guitars. These are instruments that you will probably want front and centre in your mix and it makes sense to do a superb job of compressing their individual sounds. If your mix doesn't feature such sounds, then more conventional techniques of compression will more than suffice without imposing the unnecessary layers of complexity introduced by using multiple compression bands.

Be patient with yourself as you learn to master the technique of Multiband compression. Eventually, the results will make all of that effort worthwhile.

So far, we've looked at the history and functions of compressors, together with basic and advanced techniques of compression. We have also discussed how your goals in music production can be achieved through utilising different types of compression.

This information has been consolidated into *Table 6.1* below, which can also be downloaded from our website at https://compression.producers.guide, along with other helpful summaries:

Table 6.1: A decision-making framework for which compression technique to use.

I want my sound to...	Consider...
Be more harmonically rich	A vintage compressor (or a vintage-modelling plugin)
Have tightly controlled dynamics	A digital compressor
Glue different elements together	Bus compression
Use an external source as a sidechain	Any compressor with a sidechain input, although you'll get more precision from a digital compressor
Have a large dynamic range, but never exceed a particular threshold	A limiter, or limiting compressor
Be tightly controlled, but still sound natural	Parallel compression
Use different compression ratios on different frequency bands	Multiband compression
Some combination of the above	Serial compression

If you were developing a smooth synthesizer lead and wanted your sound to be harmonically richer for example, you could look up this objective on Table 6.1, where you will see that either a vintage compressor or a vintage-modelling compressor would be ideal for this particular task.

Alternatively, if you were working with a vocal with a wide dynamic range and sought tight control of its intensity whilst retaining a natural sound, Table 6.1 will show you that it would be advantageous to apply parallel compression.

Chapter 7: Compression in Action

Whilst the previous Chapters have given you a thorough grounding in the theory behind compression techniques, this Chapter will focus upon some simple, practical exercises that I hope you will find useful to work through.

You can download free audio clips for this Chapter from: https://compression.producers.guide

The title of each section will tell you what kind of sample was originally used - such as a house drum loop—so that you can also create your own samples for each section and work on these instead, or indeed obtain one from any number of sources.

These scenarios will walk you through my thought processes for each type of track, and you will be able to recreate the results in your own DAW's compressor. Please note that I have used Logic Pro X's compressor for all these exercises, as its broad range of features allowed me to highlight specific techniques. It may be the case that your DAW's own compressor lacks some of these features. If so, please do not be deterred, since this Chapter is all about exploration and experimentation. Your end goal should not be to mimic my thought processes and choices, but to improve upon them, increasing your own knowledge in the process.

For each of the following exercises, I recommend you begin by following your chosen workflow method from Chapter 4 (either top-down, bottom-up or templated) then bypass your compressor, add a new one and duplicate the solution I've set out here. You can then compare these two results to discover which one you prefer.

7.1: Scenario One: The House Drum Loop

For this exercise, I wanted to compress a drum loop typically found in House music: a four on the floor beat, with kick drums, claps and hi-hats and a nice relaxed tempo of around 120BPM. The task of compressing such a sound might look easy at first glance, but can actually be surprisingly challenging. The compression should add energy, bounce and character, but must avoid causing any 'pumping' that is out of sync with drumbeat, or making the constituent sections of the percussion sound unnatural.

To achieve this, I selected a studio VCA character compressor. You will recall from Section 2.2.4 that VCAs are analogue compressors that not only add a tiny sprinkling of character to the sound, but are also fast and responsive. It is this responsiveness that I required in order to control the fast transients present in drum tracks.

The kick drum was inherently the loudest element. It was important to allow some of this peak intensity to give the kick drum power, but a lot of the excess energy needed to be compressed. Figure 7.1 shows both the kick drums and the transients before compression:

Kickdrum transients

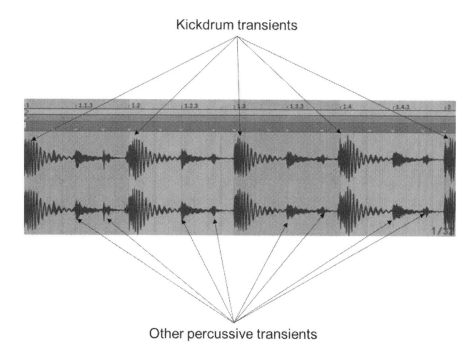

Other percussive transients

Figure 7.1: Observe the fast transients, as well as the significant peaks created by the kick drum.

I used the top-down approach for this drum loop, which meant setting an inf:1 Ratio and a Threshold 25dB below the peak, to ensure that the Attack and Release was timed correctly.

I found that at 12ms Attack and around 125ms Release, the drum track started to pump rhythmically in time with the beat, and the peak of the transients passed through the compressor unhindered, giving the drum track a powerful bounce, whilst maintaining the gentle aggression of the kick drum. Interestingly, 125ms was roughly the value of a 1/8th beat at the tempo of the drum beat.

When gradually reducing the Ratio and increasing Threshold, a -10dB Threshold and 8:1 Ratio seemed to work fairly well, with roughly 3dB of Make Up gain to balance the input and output levels. The addition of some soft Distortion added to the character of the sound.

Despite this, some unnatural 'pumping' was still audible in the upper registers. I first tried decreasing the Ratio, but I felt it inhibited the compression too much. On this basis, the compromise I arrived at was to decrease the Wet amount down to around 33%. This New York style parallel compression accomplished exactly what I wanted — harsh compression to add to the energy and character, but with a lot of space left to allow the sound to breathe.

The settings I chose are shown in Figure 7.2:

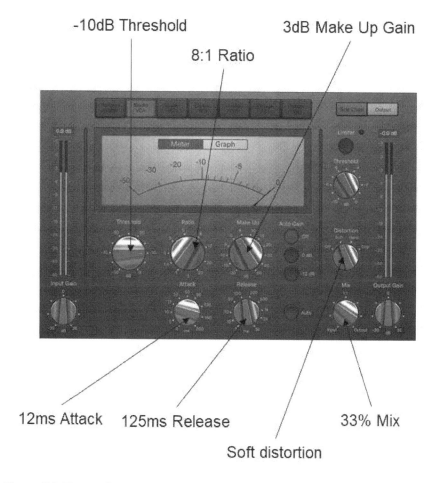

-10dB Threshold   3dB Make Up Gain

8:1 Ratio

12ms Attack   125ms Release   33% Mix

Soft distortion

Figure 7.2: The settings I chose for a House music drum loop on Logic Pro X's compressor.

Other compression settings I would consider for this drumbeat include:

1. Clean, digital compression for a very subtle effect.

2. Lower Ratio and higher Attack, to let the beat 'breathe' even more.

3. Harsh Distortion and higher Wet amount, for a pronounced, distorted sound.

7.2: Scenario Two: The Bass Guitar

For this scenario, I compressed a cleanly recorded bass guitar track. This sound was dry, in other words, no significant effects had been added to it. The sound I sought was fairly straightforward to achieve, but also just one of a multitude of available options; it could have been taken in several directions. For the purpose of this exercise however, I focussed on bringing power and character to this bass. I wanted it to shine. I therefore picked a vintage FET compressor.

You'll recall that FET compressors respond quickly and add lots of desirable warmth and colour. Using the bottom-up method of tweaking time before dynamics, I chose a slow Attack (around 50ms) and reasonably slow Release (around 500ms) so that the plucks of the bass strings could push through. After these initial string-plucks however, I wanted the compressor to clamp down hard on the sound.

For this purpose I used a -20dB Threshold with a 7:1 Ratio. This was because much of the signal was above this Threshold and it would therefore be compressed. I then added a small amount of soft Distortion to introduce a touch more character.

Finally, I added some Auto gain, decreasing the Output gain to match the input signal.

Avoiding 'pump' had been a huge concern when I was compressing the drum beat in the previous example, due to the sheer intensity of the transients, whereas in this instance I was more concerned with sustaining an unrelenting, forward energy.

Compressing this guitar resulted in a far flatter dynamic range when compared with the sound of a bassist playing naturally, but the result was warmer, more powerful, and would sit comfortably within a mix.

The configuration I chose is shown in Figure 7.3:

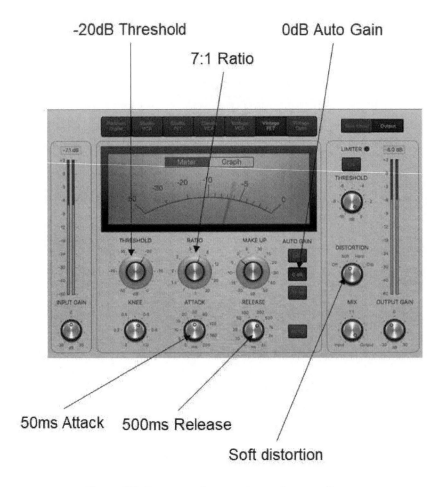

-20dB Threshold

7:1 Ratio

0dB Auto Gain

50ms Attack   500ms Release

Soft distortion

Figure 7.3: Compression used on a bass guitar.

When you listen to the compressed version, you will notice that the compression has now significantly increased the degree of hiss present on the recording. This is because we have applied Gain reduction - thereby bringing the level of the guitar closer to that of the background noise - and then applied Make Up gain to increase the intensity of the entire sound. How you would handle this is up to you as a producer. I feel the hiss would work well in a mix, but if you preferred a cleaner sound you could consider digital compression, sacrificing some character for clarity.

For this bass guitar, I could have also followed the more traditional route of compression with no Distortion. This would have imbued the bass with subtle presence and character without departing too much from the bassist's own playing style.

7.3: Scenario Three: The Vocoded Guitar

The sound I compressed for this exercise was a guitar played through a vocoder. This was a unique sound, luminous and expressive. Its dynamic range was huge, as you can see in Figure 7.4. This meant that it would be at high risk of being drowned out in any mix:

Figure 7.4: The dynamic range of the vocoded guitar.

On this basis, the compression had to accomplish three goals:

1. To highlight the sound's luminosity - I therefore didn't want too much colouring.
2. To decrease the dynamic range without dampening the transients too much.
3. To preserve the expressiveness, which meant I was seeking a fast response.

I accordingly chose a Studio VCA compressor, because it could be tight and responsive to the peaks in volume without adding much of its own colour to the sound. I used the bottom-up method for this, in other words, time before dynamics.

Since I needed some initial peaks to come through uncompressed, I set a medium-long Attack (30ms) and a medium Release (110ms).

Despite being low by usual standards, I set the Threshold to -40dB. This would have been equivalent to -25dB or so, on a sound with louder peaks.

I then combined this with a 3.25:1 Ratio. Under ordinary circumstances this would have been too harsh, but the sound had so much space and breathing-room that the results were successful.

This harsh compression allowed me to add 7.5dB of Make Up gain to match the input and output volumes. The result was a sound that was fuller, had more presence and body, but maintained its unique, delicate luminosity.

The configuration I chose is shown in Figure 7.5:

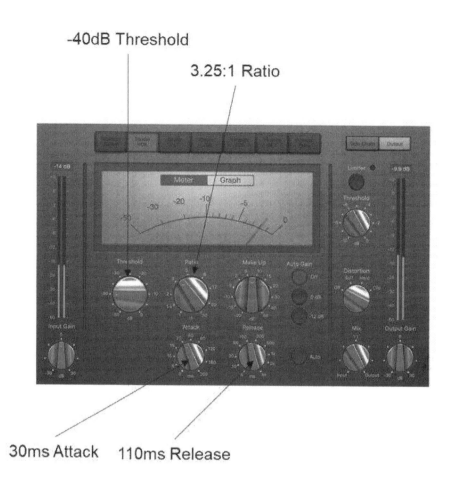

-40dB Threshold

3.25:1 Ratio

30ms Attack   110ms Release

Figure 7.5: The chosen compression on the vocoded guitar.

Were I to compress this sound again, there are two further ideas I might consider:

1. Increasing the Input gain so that the peak is 0dB and adding some Auto Gain to further flatten the dynamic range. Alternatively, in the absence of Auto Gain, I would increase the output gain of the compressor so that its peak showed at 0dB on the mixer.

2. Using traditional parallel compression with a far harsher Ratio, to significantly reduce the dynamic range whilst retaining the expressiveness of the track.

7.4: Scenario Four: The 303

For this example, I compressed a dry Roland 303 bassline loop. The Roland 303 is a classic, quirky synthesizer that needs to be treated with respect. Much of its character is expressed through its brash filters, which create an aggressive, elasticised sound with subtle filter pops and clicks, hence it was not an easy sound to compress.

The two main issues I encountered were:

1. The uncompressed sound was somewhat lacking in drive, character and aggression.

2. The accented notes (driven by enabling the 'Accent' feature on the 303's sequencer) were considerably higher in intensity than the non-accented notes, as shown in Figure 7.6:

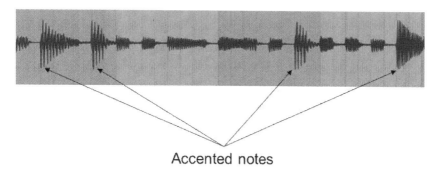

Accented notes

Figure 7.6: Accented notes in the Roland 303 pattern.

This created a bit of a conundrum. I desired the warmth, character and distortion of a vintage compressor, but I also wanted the clinical precision of a modern digital compressor. The solution was to harness both serial compression and parallel compression.

I therefore chose a chain of two compressors: a digital compressor to reduce the dynamic range, plus a vintage VCA to add subtle colouring.

I placed the digital compressor first in the signal chain to control the dynamics before colouring the sound with the VCA. This made more sense than trying to compensate for any loss of rhythmic aggression using a vintage compressor not designed for that purpose.

My settings for each compressor clearly show the intent to use it as a distinctly separate tool.

The first device - the digital compressor—was chosen for the clean, precise dynamic range reduction I was seeking. I used 0ms Attack, and around 200ms Release, allowing me to follow the bottom-up compression method. I then added a -12dB Threshold, Hard Knee, and a 5:1 Ratio for dynamic range reduction. This was compensated for by 8dB of Make Up gain.

Whilst these harsh measures controlled the sound well, the result sounded slightly too flat. On this basis, I set the compressor to 61% Wet to allow a small amount of the 303's natural dynamic range through, as seen in Figure 7.7:

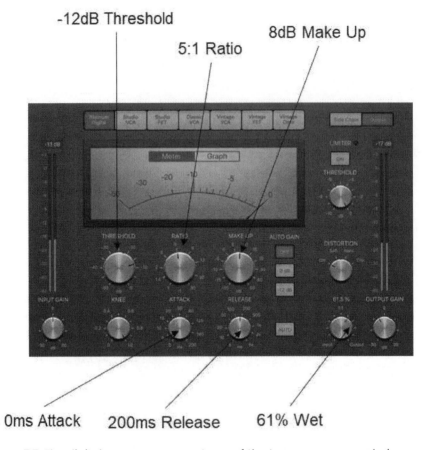

Figure 7.7: The digital compressor—part one of the two-compressor chain.

At this point I introduced the second device, the vintage VCA, to add character. I again opted for a 0ms Attack and 200ms Release and used the bottom-up approach to set the remaining parameters. I chose a -35dB Threshold to capture the entirety of the sound, Soft Knee to eliminate any artefacts in the character, and a harsh 6.5:1 Ratio. This required 7.5dB of Make Up gain, so that the input level matched that of the output.

Finally, I wanted to give the 303 additional body and character, so I added Clip Distortion, although this necessitated moving the Wet/Dry to 50/50 (or 1:1) to obtain the right amount. Clip Distortion at 50% Wet added more character than Hard Distortion at 100% Wet.

You can see the settings for this compressor in Figure 7.8:

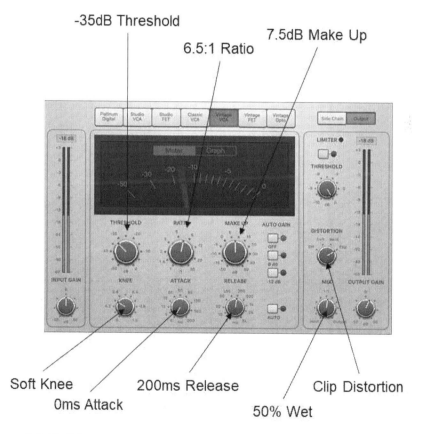

Figure 7.8: The Vintage VCA compressor: part two of the compressor chain.

If you were using a different DAW to Logic Pro X, you could probably achieve similar results using a Distortion or Saturation plugin, in place of the Vintage VCA.

Alternative techniques I would consider for compressing this 303 would include:

1. Very mild digital compression to somewhat reduce the dynamic range, allowing the natural character of the 303 to shine through.

2. Using a Distortion plugin or Tape Saturation first, only adding compression as a Limiter on the highest peaks of the sound.

7.5: Scenario Five: The Instrument Bus

This scenario involved compressing an instrument bus composed of three primary melodic elements within a track: a bassline, stabs, and a string note.

The primary purpose of compression in this case was to reduce to the dynamic range slightly to 'glue' the instruments together and maintain their collective character.

For this I chose a digital compressor which - as you will recall - is the most responsive compressor type and one that adds the least colour. I employed the top-down method, seeking quite soft compression. I arrived at this using a -22dB Threshold with a 2:1 Ratio, a 30ms Attack to preserve the transients and a 500ms Release to maintain the pressure of the compressor. This allowed me sufficient room to add 6dB of Make Up gain.

The graph on the compressor display shown in Figure 7.9 indicates that although the amount of gain reduction is small, the mix is now slightly clearer. This is because the compression has highlighted the transients and created a subtle amount of rhythmic interaction between the elements of the mix:

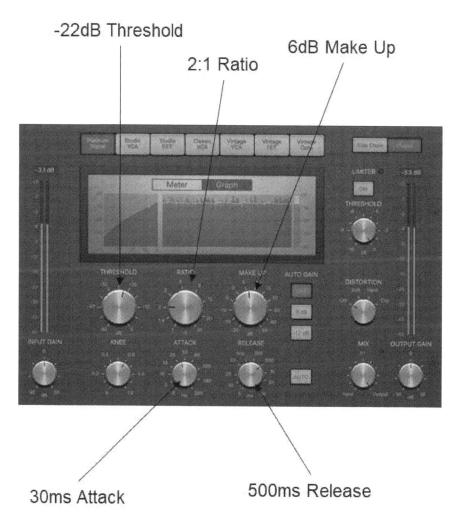

Figure 7.9: The bus compression settings chosen.

Alternative applications of compression to this sound could include:

1. Soft compression with added Distortion to enhance the sound's character.

2. Harsher compression with shorter Attack and Release to generate a little more rhythmic 'bounce'.

7.6: Scenario Six: The EDM lead

The sound used for this was an EDM lead, similar to a Roland Supersaw. The requirements for this lead were fairly obvious. EDM is known for brash, harsh, in-your-face sound design; as the lead, it had to take centre stage. Already a screaming, serrated supersaw, all this needed was some enhancement.

Because I wanted plenty of warmth and character, I initially tried optical/tube compression, but this vintage compressor dampened the energy of the higher end of the sound a little too much, depriving it of its essential brashness. Instead, the classic VCA proved the most effective for the task. It is modelled on the vintage DBX160 compressor, well known for its aggressive character. Being an emulation of a classic compressor, the dynamic range controls were limited to Threshold, Ratio and Make Up gain.

I wanted this lead to be flattened by compression and re-built to be even harsher, using Make Up gain. On this basis, I went for a low Threshold of -30dB, an aggressive Ratio of 14:1 and automatic Make Up gain of -12dB, although I had to reduce the Output gain to create parity between the Input and Output levels. The most important element, however, was the Clip Distortion as shown in

Figure 7.10, which added to the crispness of the lead without introducing undesirable characteristics:

-30dB Threshold

14:1 Ratio

-12dB Auto Gain

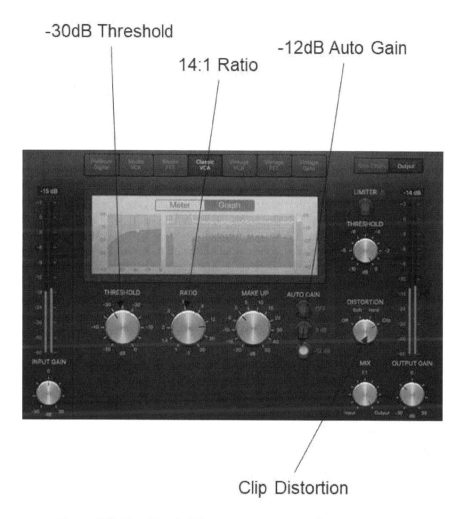

Clip Distortion

Figure 7.10: The Classic VCA compressor used for an EDM lead.

The resulting flatness and harshness of this compressed lead perfectly encapsulated the innovative EDM sound.

Other options for compression of this sound that I would consider include:

1. Subtle digital compression to further tighten the dynamic ranges, allowing the option to increase its intensity within the mix.
2. Sidechain compression from the kick drum, to give the lead a 'bounce'.

I hope you've found these exercises useful, and that your confidence in working with compression as a production tool has improved as a result of trying them out in person. The exercises were deliberately chosen to provide scenarios comparable to those you'll encounter within your own music production career. The process of compressing a sequenced synthesizer line will be very similar to that of compressing a 303, for example, and compressing a percussion track will be much the same as compressing a drum loop.

I recommend that you use this Chapter as a starting point in your compression journey, and take the time to find or create further audio samples to compress in order to increase your experience. The more you practice, the better your results will be.

As you continue to build your knowledge of compression, you will eventually gain a strong, intuitive 'feel' for what is required in any situation. At this point, compression will become instinctive and you'll begin to arrive at your own signature approach to the fascinating art of compression.

Chapter 8: Upward Compression and Multiband Dynamics

In this Chapter we'll be exploring two often overlooked compression techniques that can vastly broaden your repertoire of control over the dynamics of your sound.

8.1: Upward Compression and Expansion

Both upward and downward compression reduce the dynamic range of a sound, but this is achieved through two opposite approaches. Whereas the downward compression that we've looked at so far in this book applies gain reduction to sounds that breach the Threshold, upward compression increases the intensity of sounds below the Threshold. In other words, downward compression makes the loudest parts of the waveform quieter, whilst upward compression makes the quietest parts louder. Figure 8.1 illustrates this:

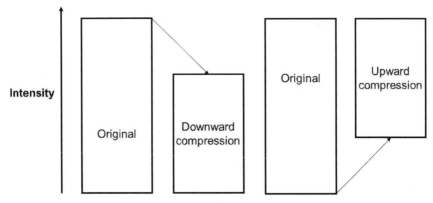

Figure 8.1: The difference between downward and upward compression. Note how downward compression reduces the intensity of the louder sounds, whereas upward compression increases the intensity of the quieter sounds.

To compare downward and upward compression, Figure 8.2 depicts downward compression and upward compression together:

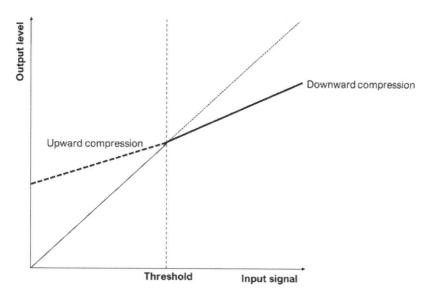

Figure 8.2: Downward and upward compression together. Notice how upward compression increases the intensity of sounds below the Threshold.

You might assume that the difference between downward and upward compression isn't particularly important; what does the direction matter, provided you're reducing the dynamic range? Think about it in practice, however.

Imagine monitoring a vocal recording for example, where some of the higher notes are too loud. In this situation you would apply downward compression to reduce the biggest peaks, and lift the overall level using Make Up gain. Because you would only apply compression to those volume peaks, most of the vocal track would remain unaffected.

Upward compression meanwhile, would keep those peaks in place and try to push everything *under* the Threshold to a higher intensity, which in effect would be most of the vocal track

Upward compression is useful when you wish to increase the intensity of everything *around* the transients. For example, you may have a live drum track, and want to increase the intensity of the recording's natural reverberation. By using upward compression, you can leave the transients of the drum hits in place, but make the reverberation more audible.

In addition to downward and upward compression, there is another form of compression that achieves the opposite to compression as we usually understand it: this is expansion. Simply put, instead of reducing the dynamic range, expansion increases it.

As with normal compression, there are two types of expansion: downward expansion and upward expansion.

Downward expansion expands the dynamic range by making sounds below the Threshold even quieter. Upward expansion expands the dynamic range by making sounds above the Threshold even louder. In both cases, the difference between the intensity of the quietest and the loudest sounds increases. This can be seen in Figure 8.3:

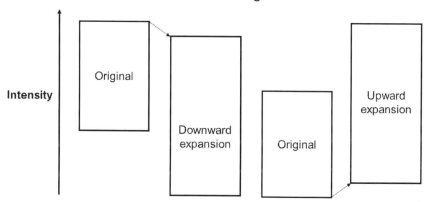

Figure 8.3: Downward and upward expansion.

Downward expansion can be used to increase the intensity of the transients relative to the noise floor, by reducing the intensity of sounds below the Threshold. Again, imagine a live drum recording. Downward expansion would be useful if you wanted to decrease the intensity of the recorded room noise, leaving the transients loud and clear.

Upward expansion on the other hand, can be used to increase the intensity of the transients themselves. In the example of the live drum track, it would boost the intensity of the drums being struck. In a music production context, this effect initially seems similar to that of downward expansion, until you factor in the use of a slower Attack setting. A slower Attack setting would mean the drum hit would now trigger a delayed expansion, increasing the loudness of the sounds that come directly after it, thereby highlighting the resonance of the drums after being struck.

Whilst upward compression and upward expansion are good in theory, they carry the inherent risk of including undesirable elements, such as breath noises and even ambient sounds from the studio environment, such as the backing track being played through the singer's headphones. You could end up with a recording that sounded strange and unnatural.

When trying to create an accurate, conventional recording of a musical performance therefore, it doesn't make a lot of sense to apply upward compression, except in small amounts and to make quite specific tweaks.

That being said, the most creative music producers often want to explore original, novel and even startling sound textures. What if highlighting the artefacts that accidentally result from upward compression could be viewed as a desirable outcome? What if we *wanted* our music to sound unnatural, and designing our sound to be counterintuitive and illogical is the very element necessary to push our music to the next level? For the innovative producer, upward compression and upward expansion can offer a doorway into unique and unusual sound textures.

You can review a summary of the four compression types in Table 8.1:

Table 8.1: Types of compression

Type	Effect on Dynamic Range	Method
Downward compression	Reduction	Reduction in intensity of sounds above the threshold (i.e. louder)
Downward expansion	Increase	Reduction in intensity of sounds below the threshold (i.e. quieter)
Upward compression	Reduction	Increase in intensity of sounds below the threshold (i.e. quieter)
Upward expansion	Increase	Increase in intensity of sounds above the threshold (i.e. louder)

These days, upward compression and upward expansion are not routinely found as standalone plugins, in the way that downward compression is. Instead, they are often packaged up within an extremely powerful plugin that combines upward compression with downward compression across multiple frequency bands. This effect is called Multiband Dynamics.

8.2: Multiband Dynamics

In this section we'll explore the various uses of multiband dynamic compression (from the subtle to the wild) together with the science behind it, so that you can understand what it's doing and how it's being done.

At the time of writing Multiband Dynamics can be found in Ableton, Studio One and Pro Tools.

To provide some background history, one of the preset patches in Ableton's Multiband Dynamics plugin was known as OTT. This patch became so popular that eventually Xfer Records - the brilliant minds behind the Serum software synthesizer - created a free standalone OTT plugin to give non-Ableton users the opportunity to experience the effect. As a consequence, the terms Multiband Dynamics and OTT are often used interchangeably in music production circles, although Multiband Dynamics per se is actually a more nuanced tool, with additional features. Despite this, the OTT plugin is essential if you don't have access to a Multiband Dynamics unit within your own DAW. At the time of writing, this freeware is available from: https://xferrecords.com/freeware

When employed subtly, Multiband Dynamics can add smoothness and warmth to a sound. It can be used as a tool to even-up the dynamic range of a vocal track, or to fit drums more comfortably into a mix.

When used brutally, it can make sounds squelch and growl. Pushed to its limits, it can add the degree of mayhem that is sometimes required to create a unique sound.

Let's begin with the plugins. Figure 8.4 depicts Ableton's Multiband Dynamics plugin:

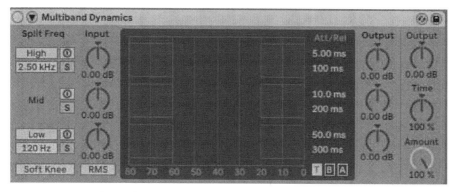

Figure 8.4: Ableton's Multiband Dynamics plugin.

Figure 8.5 shows Xfer's OTT:

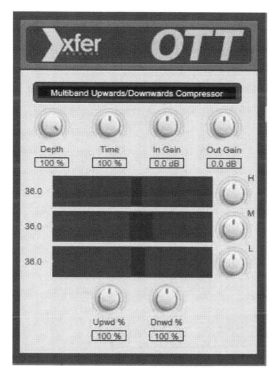

Figure 8.5: Xfer's OTT plugin.

Both perform similar functions. We'll start by exploring their features, beginning with OTT, as shown in Figure 8.6:

Figure 8.6: Four pots in Xfer's OTT plugin, explained below.

The top area of the OTT plugin covers four functions:

1. Depth refers to the depth of compression. This works in the same manner as Wet/Dry and can be used for parallel compression.

2. Time works similarly to the Attack and Decay functions on compressors and controls the speed at which the compressor works. Whereas Ableton's compressor permits individual time settings on each channel - just like a normal compressor - the Xfer plugin only allows for a vague time to be set, ranging from 0% to 100%. According to my own tests, this allows you to set an Attack ranging from approximately 0ms to around 1,500ms — although please note, this is a very rough estimate.

3. In Gain works as an amplifier before the sound enters the compressor for processing. This is helpful when you want to alter the intensity of your sound prior to compression.

4. Out Gain works as an amplifier as your sound leaves the compressor, so that you can balance your incoming and outgoing levels just as you would with a traditional downward compressor.

Ableton's Multiband Dynamics plugin possesses much the same functions, but with additional layers of complexity. I have marked the plugin in Figure 8.7 with the elements that correspond with the four parameters described above. These are:

1. Depth (Amount on Multiband Dynamics).
2. Time (Attack and Release on Multiband Dynamics).
3. In Gain (Input on Multiband Dynamics).
4. Out Gain (Output on Multiband Dynamics).

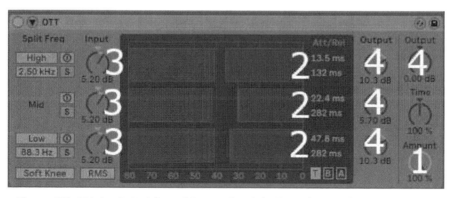

Figure 8.7: Ableton's Multiband Dynamics, labelled with the four functions it shares with Xfer's OTT above.

Unlike OTT, Ableton offers the option to change the Input Gain and Attack/Release speed across each band.

Now let's look at the bands that make it a multiband compressor. These are High, Mid and Low. These bands are depicted on both the OTT and Ableton's Multiband Dynamics plugins in Figure 8.8:

Figure 8.8: A comparison of Xfer OTT and Ableton Live, detailing the three available bands for compression.

Ableton's Multiband Dynamics plugin has crossovers, allowing the user to select the bandings of the High, Medium and Low frequencies, but the High, Medium and Low bands of Xfer OTT are fixed. I have analysed Xfer OTT's plugin's bands and found the following rough frequency banding for them:

- High: 2.4kHz or above.
- Mid: 128Hz to 2.4kHz.
- Low: 128Hz or lower.

These frequency bands are aimed quite firmly at electronic music producers. The Low band in particular is well-suited to processing sub-bass and the lower end of a kick drum.

You will see in Figure 8.9 that each of the three bands on Ableton's Multiband Dynamics contains blocks of colour, situated either side of a dark centre:

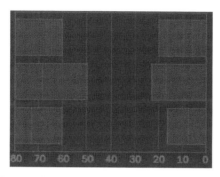

Figure 8.9: The display on the Multiband Dynamics plugin.

The dark centre represents areas where compression does not apply, because the compression Thresholds are either side of them. These Thresholds are called the Above and Below Thresholds, as shown in Figure 8.10:

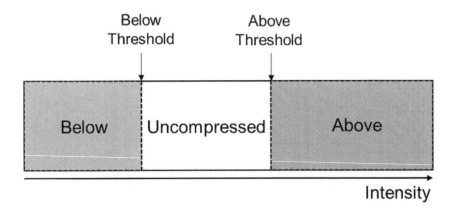

Figure 8.10: The Below and Above Thresholds, as displayed on multiband dynamics plugins.

Within Xfer's OTT plugin, all audio signals under the Below Threshold receive upward compression, all audio signals above the Above Threshold will receive downward compression and all audio signals whose intensity lies within the middle area will remain uncompressed, as shown in Figure 8.11:

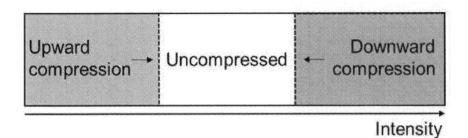

Figure 8.11: The results of the Above and Below Thresholds on the Xfer OTT plugin.

The same function on the OTT plugin is illustrated in Figure 8.12:

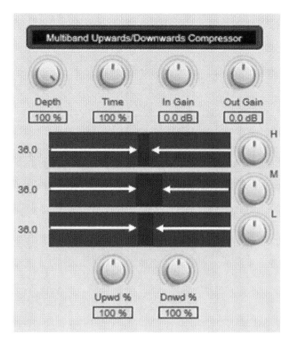

Figure 8.12: The effect of the compression bands within the Xfer OTT plugin.

It is worth noting that Ableton's Multiband Dynamics supports Ratios below the value of 1, in both its Above and Below areas. This complicates things a little, because it means that both areas can equally provide forms of upwards and downwards compression, as can be seen in Figure 8.13:

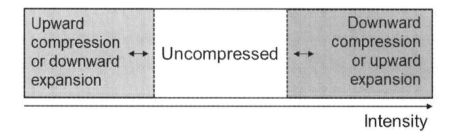

Figure 8.13: The types of compression possible with Ableton's Multiband Dynamics plugin. Compare this to Figure 8.11, displaying how Xfer OTT offers

downward compression only in the left zone and upward compression only in the right zone.

This is further explained in Table 8.2 below:

Table 8.2: The result of ratios below 1 in Ableton Multiband Dynamics.

Area	Ratios above 1	Ratios below 1
Above Threshold	Downward compression	Upward expansion
Below Threshold	Upward compression	Downward expansion

You can use Ableton's Multiband Dynamics as a traditional 'downward' multiband compressor by dragging the Upward zones to the left out of sight. As you can see in Figure 8.14, only downward compression will now apply to the signal:

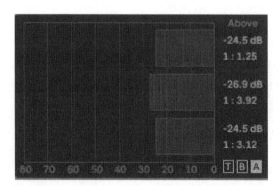

Figure 8.14: Ableton's Multiband Dynamics set to add Downward compression only.

Conversely, dragging the Downward zones to the rightmost edges means that only upward compression is applied, as you can see in Figure 8.15:

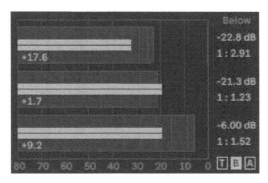

Figure 8.15: Upward expansion being applied.

This combination of upward and downward compression means that the Ratios used in Multiband Dynamics can be counterintuitive.

Remember that when the Ratio is above 1, the Ratio in downward compression defines the degree of gain reduction applied when a sound breaches the Threshold defined by the Above Thresholds. Meanwhile, the Ratio in upward compression defines the amount of upward compression when a sound breaches the Below Thresholds. This means that a 2:1 Ratio *increases* the gain.

To illustrate this, let's look at what happens if we use the Multiband Dynamics plugin on a sawtooth pulse. As can be seen in Figure 8.16, the Above and Below Thresholds create distinct 'zones' of compression:

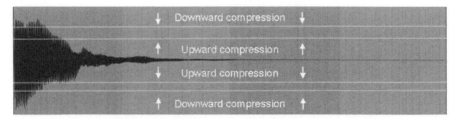

Figure 8.16: The 'zones' of compression created by the two Thresholds.

Applying Multiband Dynamics to this sound drastically changes the waveform, as depicted in Figure 8.17:

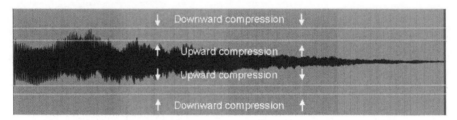

Figure 8.17: A reverberated sawtooth with the OTT plugin applied.

You can immediately see two primary effects from its application:

1. The intensity of the transient at the start of the sawtooth sound has been drastically reduced by downward compression.
2. The intensity of the reverb tail has been massively increased by upward compression.

The process has essentially 'squeezed' the sound. Notice how the original sound follows the norms of a reverberated pulse - the initial transient is followed by the rapidly decreasing intensity of the reverb tail. Multiband Dynamics compression meanwhile seems to increase a sound's intensity *after* it has elapsed, resulting in an unearthly beast of a sound.

These illustrations demonstrate the effect of Multiband Dynamics on the intensity of a sound's waveform, but they do not show the psychoacoustic effect - how the sound is perceived by the listener. The synthetic pulse and subsequent reverb tail of the original sound comes across like a pulse being played in a large reverberant room, such as an empty Community Hall. The compressed sound on the other hand, with its reverb tail now slightly louder than the initial pulse, doesn't accord with our mental expectations of ordinary audio envelopes, because natural environments do not reverberate sounds more loudly than the initial impulse that caused them. This makes the sound *feel* artificial, but also imbues it with a unique and attention-grabbing quality.

8.3: Further Features of Multiband Dynamics

Ableton's Multiband Dynamics features some additional controls that are not currently available on OTT. We'll take a look at these below.

1. The Activator and Solo buttons. The Activator buttons: activate or deactivate compression on the High, Mid and Low bands. To switch off compression in this way allows that particular band to pass through the compressor unaltered. The Solo buttons, meanwhile: allow you to select an individual band that excludes the others. If you were to Solo the mid band, for example,

the mid band is the only one that would be allowed to pass through the compressor.

The Activator and Solo buttons are illustrated in Figure 8.18:

Activator and
Solo buttons

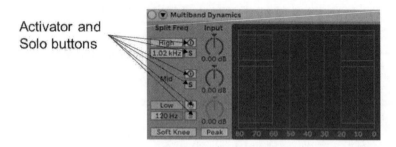

Figure 8.18: Activator and Solo buttons.

2. The Band On/Off buttons. These buttons: High and Low also turn the high and low bands on and off, but unlike the Activator buttons, when a band is switched to Off, it merges with the middle band and you will see this reflected in the display. If you were to switch both bands off, the effects unit would essentially become a single-band compressor, working across all frequencies using the settings of the Mid band. The Band Activator buttons are shown in Figure 8.19:

Band activator
buttons

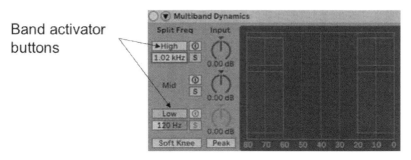

Figure 8.19: The Band Activator buttons. Note how the Low band is switched off.

3. Knee and Peak/RMS. As described in Chapter 3, Knee governs how the Ratio is applied to sounds breaching the Threshold. Hard Knee follows the Ratio precisely, whereas Soft Knee relaxes the compression Ratio slightly when breaches of the Threshold are fairly minor. Peak/RMS compression is as described in Chapter 3. Whereas Peak means the compressor responds to the short peaks within a signal, RMS is more subtle, averaging the signal over time to create a softer degree of compression. These buttons are shown in Figure 8.20:

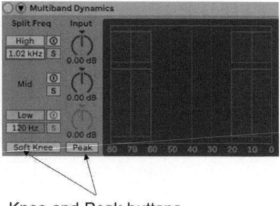

Knee and Peak buttons

Figure 8.20: Knee and Peak buttons.

Ableton's Multiband Dynamics is clearly a more nuanced tool than Xfer's OTT. However, Xfer's free OTT plugin is perfectly suitable for meeting the needs of most applications.

Chapter 9: Practical Examples of Multiband Dynamics

In this Chapter I will demonstrate the application of Multiband Dynamics and OTT with some practical examples. Being diverse tools with a multiplicity of creative possibility, these uses will range from the traditional and sensible right through to the innovative and cutting-edge.

As ever, all audio samples are freely available to download from https://compression.producers.guide.

I recommend that you follow my configurations to start with and then experiment by applying your own parameters to each sound in order to explore the possibilities and familiarise yourself with these controls.

Even though Multiband Dynamics has more features than OTT, the focus of this Chapter is the similarity of their use for the purpose of upward compression. The terms *OTT* and *Multiband Dynamics* will therefore be used interchangeably throughout, since the results and process should be fully transferrable from one to the other.

9.1: Wobble Bass

A sound that started life within a few niche circles on the fringes of Garage and Grime music, wobble bass is now prevalent across many electronic music genres. It is a simple sound, combining a huge synthesized bass with a filter programmed by an LFO to create a rhythmic pulse. Just like OTT, it came about through a careful exploration of parameters — a single LFO dial opened up a world of wonders.

Although simple to construct, achieving maximum impact with a wobble bass can be tricky. Fortunately, Multiband Dynamics can help us enhance the sound in exactly the right way.

One of the main issues you will encounter when programming a wobble bass is its lack of presence. Ideally, it should be the strongest element of the mix, but without careful handling it can lack the intensity and power necessary to bring it to the very forefront of the mix.

Professionally produced tracks often place a great deal of emphasis on the mid-upper frequency range of wobble basses. This is because although they are basses, they derive much of their presence from these higher frequencies. Whilst the original wobble bass shown in the spectrum analysis in Figure 9.1 appears quite powerful, it is actually fairly subdued:

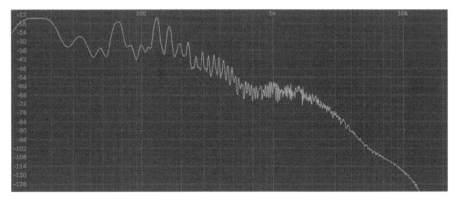

Figure 9.1: A spectrum analysis of the wobble bass.

You could potentially mitigate this by using EQ to emphasise these mid-upper frequencies, but doing so still won't give you the strength and power you require.

Multiband Dynamics (in this case, the OTT plugin) will imbue the wobble bass with much greater presence; the bass will sound fatter, fuller and more aggressive. The spectrum analysis shown in Figure 9.2 illustrates this:

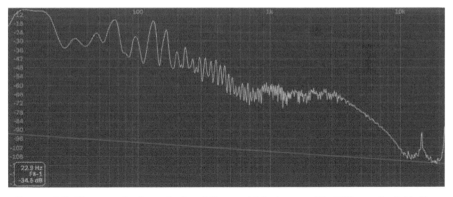

Figure 9.2: The spectral analysis of the wobble bass with OTT applied. Notice the increase in upper harmonics.

Let's analyse how this effect is achieved. Figure 9.3 shows the configuration of the OTT plugin:

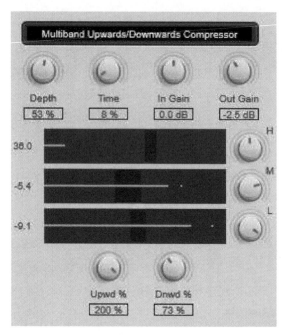

Figure 9.3: An example of an OTT plugin in action on a wobble bass.

1. You'll notice that the Out Gain (in the top right) has been reduced by 2.5dB. Remember the principles of objective compression discussed in Chapter 4 - we need to make sure we're improving the sound, not simply making it louder. This reduction has matched the input level of the sound with its output level, thus ensuring that a real difference is being made to it.

2. Time has been reduced to 8%. This is so that the plugin responds quickly to the individual wobbles.

3. H has been kept the same, M has been increased to 3 o'clock and L increased to 5 o'clock. This has been done to bring more presence to the lower and middle ends of the sound.

4. Much of the presence applied to the wobble bass results from moving the Below Threshold of the H band upwards. This drags more of the high end of the sound upwards, increasing the high-frequency growl between the main trainsients.

5. Upwd % has been increased to 200% and Dnwd % to 73%. This is to create extreme upward compression.

6. To prevent clipping caused by this degree of compression, Depth is now at 53%, essentially using OTT as parallel compression.

This is an exemplary use of OTT on a simple instrument, and the results are exceptionally powerful. In the next section, we'll review how OTT can be used to affect a more complex sound.

9.2: Dub Techno Chords

As you'll probably know, Dub Techno chords are built around rich, complex sonorities such as minor chord triads, sevenths and ninths. They are heard as stabs to which lingering reverb and beautiful stereo delay are usually applied by the producer. Correctly balancing the intensity of the stabs with that of the delays however can be challenging - too wet and the original stabs will be drowned out, whilst too much feedback will cause the delay to linger unpleasantly.

OTT can assist the Dub Techno producer to both highlight these cascading, delayed chords and control the interaction between them and their effects.

OTT's upwards compression gives the delays and reverb tails more presence, whilst the subtle downward compression warms up the sound. Figure 9.4 shows how this configuration is achieved:

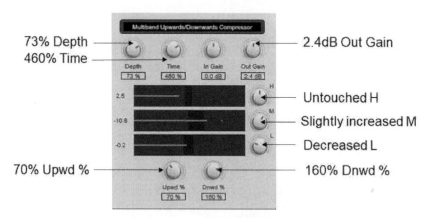

Figure 9.4: The OTT configuration used on Dub Techno chords.

In this example, I've used a fairly high Time, to allow the upward and downward compression to develop slowly and expansively. The H and M sections enhance the upper and mid areas, with the L completely removing the unwanted bass element. Turning the Upwd % to 160% increases the degree of upward compression. This highlights the individual delays, resulting in a rich, warm, complex sound, which sits beautifully in the mix.

One of the most interesting aspects of this treatment - one that you can recreate if you download the original file - is the modulation of Time. The lower the Time, the more Reverb is allowed through. This is because a higher Time value corresponds to a higher Attack value on the OTT plugin, so the compressor will wait longer before applying upward compression, thus making the Reverb more prominent. In this instance, I've chosen 460%, which seems a reasonable compromise, but there are many possibilities to be explored - in fact, modulating the Time as you would modulate a synthesizer filter can provide a whole new dimension to your sound design.

Figure 9.5 shows the chords prior to using OTT:

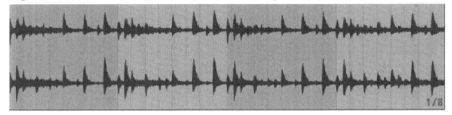

Figure 9.5: Dub Techno chords before OTT's use.

Figure 9.6, shows those same chords after using OTT:

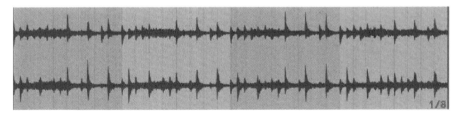

Figure 9.6: Dub Techno chords after OTT's use.

Whilst the overall waveform seems less energetic in Figure 9.6, the intensity of the delays and reverb has been increased, giving a very different feel to the sonic texture.

Using Izotope's Imager to compare the sounds in Figures 9.5 and 9.6, we can obtain a Polar Level analysis. The original chord stabs are shown in Figure 9.7, displaying the stereo distribution:

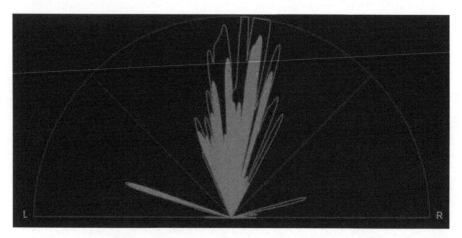

Figure 9.7: A Polar Level analysis of the original stabs.

Compare this with the Polar Level analysis of the stabs after OTT compression in Figure 9.8:

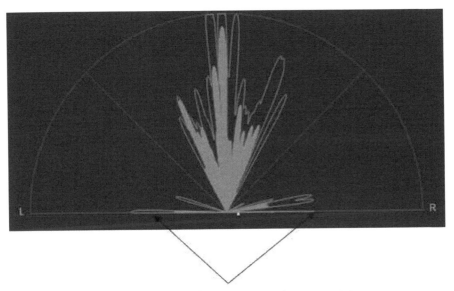

Additional stereo information

Figure 9.8: Polar Level analysis of the stabs after OTT compression.

You will see that that the sound now possesses a greater stereo width as a consequence of OTT compression. It is important to note here however that this is *not* because OTT has actually made the sound wider, but because the stereo width of this sound lies in the low-intensity delays, and their intensity has been increased by OTT's upward compression.

To summarise, OTT uses upwards compression to pull the intensity of delays upwards. This is what makes it such a great tool for any sound that relies upon the use of Stereo Delay.

9.3: Multiple Instruments - Effects Bus Glue

As we discussed in Section 5.2, compressors are well known for their ability to act as a 'glue', pulling the various different parts of a track together. In the context of bus compression, this means making disparate elements within a mix sound more like a single element. It accomplishes this through a reduction in dynamic range, one of the key methods our ears use to distinguish different sounds from one another.

Imagine several tracks within a mix being sent to Bus 10, meaning their signals are being duplicated and diverted to a separate channel containing effects. An example of what this would look like on Logic Pro X can be seen in Figure 9.9:

Figure 9.9: Three tracks being 'sent' to an effects bus.

You can see in Figure 9.10 that I have added OTT to the effects chain *after* the Delay and Reverb effects. This is to glue together the delay and reverb that was previously added to the overall mix:

Figure 9.10: OTT added in the signal chain after the effects, essentially 'gluing' the effects together.

Doing this makes the Delay and Reverb sound like a separate track in itself, and works far better than three channel delays and reverbs being used independently. This is because the OTT creates interactions in the dynamic ranges of the different elements, creating a 'glue'.

Whilst this kind of 'gluing' compression is often used on the musical elements themselves rather than their effects, in this instance I wanted to keep the musical elements separate, only 'gluing' the effects together to make the layers sound closer to one another.

Because I wanted to use OTT as a 'glue', I set it to immediate Attack (0% Time). To set the Time any higher would have meant allowing some peaks to occur without any compression, reducing the consistency between them. I also turned Upwd % to 150%. This increased the degree of upward expansion being applied to the Delay and Reverb artefacts, as can be seen in Figure 9.11:

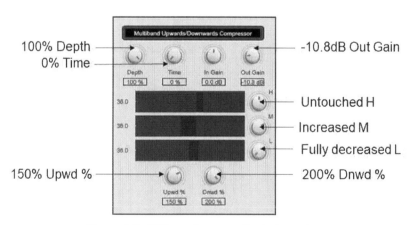

Figure 9.11: OTT used as an effects bus glue.

Because the combination of Delay and Reverb was producing some unwanted booming bass frequencies, I brought down the Low to reduce their occurrence. I also set the Mid Threshold quite high by reducing the amount of downward compression applied to it, since much of the frequency content lay within that band.

The outcome of this was a far more consistent sound. The individual instruments sat nicely within their own sonic space, whilst the effects of the bus OTT sounded like a separate layer.

9.4: Drum Break

Older drum break samples offer particular challenges due to their large dynamic range. This can prove both a blessing and a curse, because whilst it can imbue them with a lot of energy, it also makes them very difficult to control. Jungle producers back in the 1990s loved the bouncy energy of a dynamic drum break, but modern producers tend to prefer one with a lower dynamic range because it is simpler to manage and will fit more easily into a densely layered mix.

For this example, I have used the famous Amen break - easily the most recognisable drum break in the history of electronic music.

The classic Amen has a typically wide dynamic range, as shown in Figure 9.12. This reflects not only the original conditions under which the break was recorded in 1969, but also the way that records were mastered before the race for the loudest possible mix began:

Figure 9.12: The waveform of the Amen break. Notice the wide dynamic range.

Your first thought might well be to reduce the intensity of these transients through traditional downward compression - and there would be nothing wrong with such an approach.

However, the Amen is ubiquitous in electronic music, and you may want instead to create something more modern, innovative, and interesting. In this case, we can use OTT to not only reduce the intensity of the biggest transients but also expand everything else including the quieter transients, the background noise and perhaps even the room reverberations present in the recording.

Applying extreme OTT compression transforms the Amen break into a squelchy, harsh, noisy monster, as can be seen in Figure 9.13:

Figure 9.13: The waveform of the Amen Break with harsh OTT compression applied.

In this case, I used Ableton's Multiband Dynamics plugin, starting with the OTT preset. As you can see in Figure 9.14, this preset uses a harsh degree of both upward and downward compression, with particular emphasis on High. Given this harshness, parallel compression was the best approach here, setting the Wet to around 32%, as can be seen in Figure 9.14:

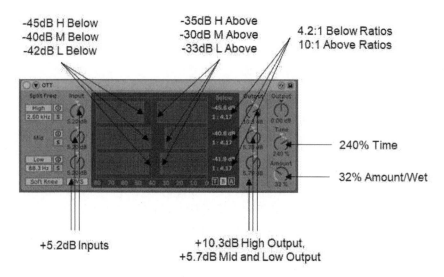

Figure 9.14: The Multiband Dynamics preset used on the Amen break.

This created a compromise – a harsh, distorted, flat Amen, but one with enough dynamism to retain the original energy that sustains the break, as depicted in Figure 9.15. Notice that the original transients have now returned:

Figure 9.15: The Amen break with OTT compression applied at 32% Wet; a compromise between the original and the 100% compressed version.

If your tastes are more extreme than mine, you might even prefer the sound of the Amen break at 100% Wet. The results certainly won't sound like any Amen break I've ever heard, but this only goes to further highlight the wonders of OTT: it allows the stretching of sonic dynamics to create completely new iterations. It is through just such experimentation that novel sounds are arrived at.

In the next section, we will look at an interesting use of OTT, where we'll be using it to improve a subdued, poor-quality vocal sample.

9.5: Vocal Processing

Vocals are wonderful things. Most mainstream music is still structured around them, and even the coldest, most abstract electronic music can be warmed up with a vocal touch. Simply put, they are vital to music production.

Unfortunately, vocals are also the toughest element to record successfully. Most high-quality vocals come from professional studio recordings. These are expensive to produce, and the copyright of good vocals is aggressively defended by record labels; an uncleared vocal sample in a successful track can place the unwary producer in a great deal of peril.

Because of this, a producer may opt to use vocals from free sample sites such as www.freesound.org. This is a fine idea, but these vocals often benefit from some sonic crafting to get them up to spec before use. This section deals with precisely such a vocal.

The vocal used for this example is has been processed, and uses lots of reverses over the course of the melody. Its main issue is that it can sound blunt in a mix.

As you will see in Figure 9.16, its waveform has a wide dynamic range:

Figure 9.16: The waveform of a processed vocal sample.

This means that the areas of lower intensity can tend to get lost in a mix.

The vocal also lacks essential sharpness, the frequency analysis showing a lack of higher frequency content. These are the frequencies that create a sense of clarity in a sound, as seen in Figure 9.17:

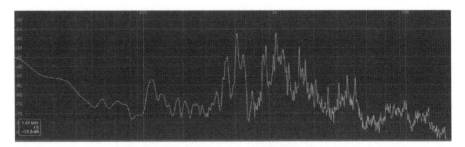

Figure 9.17: Spectrum analysis of the vocal.

To make this vocal shine, we therefore need to achieve two things:

1. Bring up the moments of lower intensity.
2. Brighten the vocal to give it clarity.

On that basis, I used Multiband Dynamics to achieve both. I demonstrate how I set about this in Figure 9.18:

-22dB H Below
-24dB M Below
-26dB L Below

-20dB H Above
-20dB M Above
-18dB L Above

8:1 H and M Below Ratios
inf:1 L Below Ratio
10:1 H and M Above Ratios
1:inf L Above Ratio

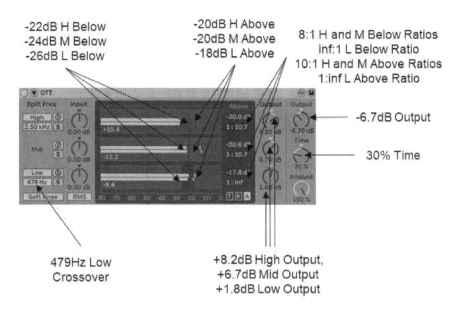

-6.7dB Output

30% Time

479Hz Low
Crossover

+8.2dB High Output,
+6.7dB Mid Output
+1.8dB Low Output

Figure 9.18: The configuration of Multiband Dynamics used to fix a vocal.

As you saw from the spectrum analysis, the middling frequency section of the vocal was around 500Hz, so I set the low crossover around that point.

I then moved the Below Thresholds up, so that Upward compression was applied to most of the vocal. On the rare occasions a transient from the vocal exceeded the Below area, it immediately transitioned to the Above section, where it met a harsh 5:1 Ratio. This meant that most of the vocal was now being compressed upwards. I then brought Time down to 30% to ensure that whilst the compression was smooth, it acted quickly. You can see the effect of this in Figure 9.19:

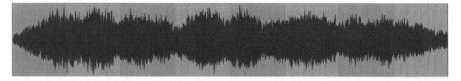

Figure 9.19: The Vocal after Multiband Dynamics.

I then increased the outputs of the Mid and High sections to bring the brightness and clarity that the vocal required. This considerably brightened up the vocal - compare the spectrum analysis in Figure 9.17 with the original in Figure 9.20:

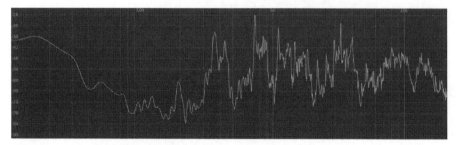

Figure 9.20: The brighter, sharper vocal. Note the peak around 20Hz—this will need to be cleaned up using EQ later.

These simple steps transformed the vocal from an interesting but unremarkable sound to a sparkling, powerful one.

There was one unintended consequence, however - the Upward compression also dragged up the intensity of the hiss at the start and end of the recording; something that will require further editing later. However, that's a small price to pay for a vivid vocal that cost nothing, sounds fantastic and won't get you into trouble!

Our next exploration of OTT will look at a classic Techno sound (and one of my personal favourites): the 909 ride cymbal.

9.6 Ride Cymbals

If you are a Techno, House, or Tech-house producer, you will be entirely familiar with the technique of using 909 ride cymbals. Their hissy, funky, rhythmic groove hovers over your mix, bringing a boost of additional energy to your sound.

This technique has been heard in electronic music for over thirty years however, and even a slightly unique take on it can give your track that extra bit of edge and spice it needs to stand out from the crowd. If you've listened to the likes of Ben Klock or Etapp Kyle, you'll have already noticed a significant degree of innovation in this field.

A small amount of OTT is all that is required to give ride cymbals some cutting edge. An example of a configuration that would achieve this is shown in Figure 9.21:

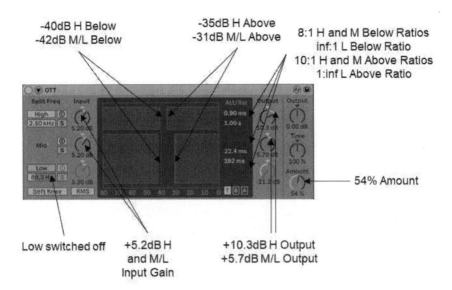

-40dB H Below
-42dB M/L Below

-35dB H Above
-31dB M/L Above

8:1 H and M Below Ratios
inf:1 L Below Ratio
10:1 H and M Above Ratios
1:inf L Above Ratio

54% Amount

Low switched off

+5.2dB H
and M/L
Input Gain

+10.3dB H Output
+5.7dB M/L Output

Figure 9.21: The Multiband Dynamics used to enhance 909 ride cymbals.

You'll see that I've cut the Low altogether, using OTT to enhance the top end, bringing the Attack down to 0.90ms so that it acts immediately. I further enhanced the sound by increasing the amount of High using the Output level.

The upward compression plays a particular role here. A great deal of hiss and interest lies between the transients of the ride cymbal; this hiss isn't usually particularly audible, but highlighting it using OTT makes the sound fascinating.

As you will see from the new waveform in Figure 9.22, the decay of the cymbal has been increased, and a lot of noise has been added:

Figure 9.22: The new ride cymbal waveform.

The result of this is a more lo-fi, more analogue-sounding ride, one that pushes its way into the mix rather than merely sitting on top of it.

In the next and final section, we'll look at the use of Multiband Dynamics to help you with something very important if you're a DJ – adding punch!

9.7: Mix Mastering

As a DJ, you will routinely record your mixes. However, when listening back to them - especially outside of the context of mixing them loudly - you may find that they lack punch, particularly if you're mixing between formats (e.g. CD and vinyl) or between tracks of a different era.

This is where Multiband Dynamics comes in.

You can add extra punch to your sound using the power of upward compression. Using upward compression to expand your lower and upper transients increases the punch of your kicks and hi-hats, giving your mixes that extra edge. This is particularly useful when you have modern tracks mixing with older tracks that have different production values.

One of the best techniques for this can be found on Ableton's website at https://www.ableton.com/en/manual/live-audio-effect-reference/. To adapt this for use in a DJ mix, I would recommend something like the following:

You can add extra punch and tighten the transients by following these steps:

1. Reduce the input volume. This creates the space within the dynamic range to expand the transients.

2. Alter the Above Thresholds so that they sit below the highest peaks. This means that the highest peaks receive some degree of downward compression. You can set these to a fairly relaxed Ratio, around 2:1, although you can vary things significantly around this. In this instance I didn't add downward compression to the H band.

3. Increase the Below Thresholds on the Low section so that they apply upward compression to more of the lower end, leaving the Mid and High in place. You can use a small amount of upward compression on these, to push the transients higher, using a Ratio of 2:1.

4. Tighten the Attack and Release times, giving the Upward element a fast Attack that would push the kickdrum higher.

5. Increase the overall volume of the Bass band to give it some extra push.

6. Slightly increase the overall volume of the High band to give it slightly more presence.

7. Increase the Output to push the volume of the overall mix higher.

This process is illustrated in Figure 9.23:

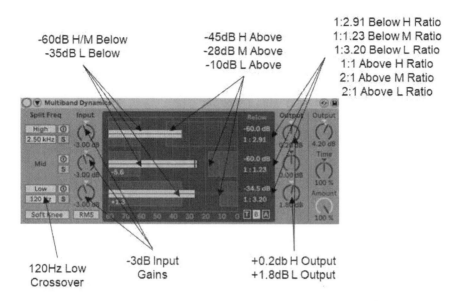

-60dB H/M Below
-35dB L Below

-45dB H Above
-28dB M Above
-10dB L Above

1:2.91 Below H Ratio
1:1.23 Below M Ratio
1:3.20 Below L Ratio
1:1 Above H Ratio
2:1 Above M Ratio
2:1 Above L Ratio

120Hz Low
Crossover

-3dB Input
Gains

+0.2db H Output
+1.8dB L Output

Figure 9.23: The Multiband Dynamics settings used on a DJ set.

This creates a much bouncier, warmer mix. So, thank you Ableton, for inspiring such a fantastic use of Multiband Dynamics.

Whether for the purposes of highlighting quieter transients in Dub Techno chords, adding power to a vocal or DJ set, or enhancing the power of ride cymbals, we've looked at a variety of uses for OTT compression. What they possess in common is that OTT has stretched, warped and enhanced these sounds. Even though it's not a traditionally natural effect, OTT is the perfect tool for creating novel, exciting, innovative sounds.

In light of this, I recommend that your ongoing practice with OTT compression is one of experimentation. Being on the cutting edge of music, there's currently very little by way of received wisdom or tradition established for its use. This frees you up to use it as a powerful tool to take your music production to the next level!

Chapter 10: Conclusion

In writing this book, I hope that I have provided you with the foundations necessary to begin using compression with skill, confidence and flair. Within its pages you have learned about the use of compression as an integral audio effect, one that is essential to the art of modern music production. You have also learned a little about its history, as well as being introduced to some of the most cutting-edge uses of compression as a tool for producing startling, amazing and stunning audio textures.

The practical exercises you have undertaken whilst studying this book will have assisted you to create a subconscious mental model of compression; one that will stay with you throughout your production career and facilitate the intuitive use of compression that is the hallmark of professional producers.

In closing, I hope this book will remain a helpful companion to you for whenever you need a point of reference. It only remains for me to wish you the very best in your exciting musical journey.

Thank you for reading!

Printed in Great Britain
by Amazon